LEADERS OF THE CIVIL WAR ERA

Robert E. Lee

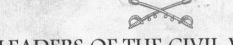

LEADERS OF THE CIVIL WAR ERA

John Brown

Jefferson Davis

Frederick Douglass

Ulysses S. Grant

Stonewall Jackson

Robert E. Lee

Abraham Lincoln

William Tecumseh Sherman

Harriet Beecher Stowe

Harriet Tubman

LEADERS OF THE CIVIL WAR ERA

Robert E. Lee

Tim McNeese

CHELSEA HOUSE
PUBLISHERS
An imprint of Infobase Publishing

ROBERT E. LEE

Copyright ©2009 by Infobase Publishing

All rights reserved. No part of this book may be reproduced or utilized in any form or
by any means, electronic or mechanical, including photocopying, recording, or by any
information storage or retrieval systems, without permission in writing from the publisher.
For information contact:

Chelsea House
An imprint of Infobase Publishing
132 West 31st Street
New York NY 10001

Library of Congress Cataloging-in-Publication Data
McNeese, Tim.
Robert E. Lee / Tim McNeese.
   p. cm. — (Leaders of the Civil War era)
Includes bibliographical references and index.
ISBN 978-1-60413-304-2 (hardcover : alk. paper)
1. Lee, Robert E. (Robert Edward) 1807–1870—Juvenile literature. 2. Generals—United
States—Biography—Juvenile literature. 3. Generals—Confederate States of America—
Biography—Juvenile literature. 4. United States. Army—Biography—Juvenile literature.
5. Confederate States of America. Army—Biography—Juvenile literature. 6. United States—
History—Civil War, 1861–1865—Juvenile literature. I. Title. II. Series.
E467.1.L4M495 2009
973.7'3092—dc22
[B]   2008044623

Chelsea House books are available at special discounts when purchased in bulk quantities
for businesses, associations, institutions, or sales promotions. Please call our Special Sales
Department in New York at (212) 967-8800 or (800) 322-8755.

You can find Chelsea House on the World Wide Web at http://www.chelseahouse.com

Series design by Erik Lindstrom
Cover design by Keith Trego

Printed in the United States of America

Bang KT 10 9 8 7 6 5 4 3 2 1

This book is printed on acid-free paper.

All links and Web addresses were checked and verified to be correct at the time of
publication. Because of the dynamic nature of the Web, some addresses and links may have
changed since publication and may no longer be valid.

CONTENTS

Introduction

Having recently turned 54 years of age and still stationed out in a remote corner of southwest Texas, Colonel Robert E. Lee began to feel homesick that late winter of 1861. Everything was changing so rapidly back East, and the lonely Virginian felt removed from the events that were taking over the country. He had worn a U.S. military uniform for 35 years, including his four years as a cadet at West Point. Out in the deserts of West Texas, he longed for his former life in Virginia, at his wife's estate at Arlington, across the Potomac River from Washington, D.C.

A CALL TO WASHINGTON

He had talked of leaving the army for several years, as far back as when he had been a lieutenant. Many of his old associates in

Although the Civil War introduced a new form of warfare with which he was not familiar, Lee was able to keep the Union Army at bay for nearly three years. A West Point alumnus and career army officer, Lee was one of the most celebrated generals in American history.

uniform, and others with whom he had not been that friendly, had given up military service, including Jefferson Davis, Thomas Jackson, William "Rosey" Rosecrans, William T. Sherman, George B. McClellan, Joseph Hooker, Ambrose Burnside, even Albert Sidney Johnston, who had previously held Lee's command over the 2nd U.S. Cavalry Regiment in Texas. He had dedicated his life to his military arts, and, it seemed to him, everyone else had left him and the U.S. Army behind.

Then in February, Robert E. Lee was suddenly called back East to Washington, D.C., although there were no clear orders or assignment. His trip to the nation's capital took three weeks. By March 1, Lee was in Washington, meeting with his superior commander, General Winfield Scott. The two men sat down to a meeting that went on for three solid hours. There is no official record of the content of their meeting, but it is assumed that the U.S. Army commander wanted to know whether Lee would support Southern secession. The country was being ripped apart by those who felt their way of life—one dependent on slavery—was threatened, especially with the election of President Abraham Lincoln. Emotions were running high across the South as states severed their political ties with the United States. Most likely, Scott encouraged Lee to stay and serve as his aide in case a war between the states unfolded.

In the spring of 1861, Scott was a man in his seventies who had seen better days as a military commander. Over the course of his nearly 50-year career, he had commanded forces through several wars, including the War of 1812 and the Mexican-American War (1846–1848). Weighing more than 300 pounds, he was now too heavy to mount a horse by himself or even walk a short distance without becoming winded. His military days were over and Scott, should war unfold, would need to be replaced by someone with adequate field experience, someone Scott could support. Lee was one of only a handful of U.S. military officers who could fill the old general's boots.

Lee left Scott's office concerned about his and his country's future. Three days later, on March 4, Lincoln took the oath of office on the west portico of the U.S. Capitol and became the sixteenth president of the United States. Seven states had already seceded from the Union, including Texas, where Lee commanded the 2nd Cavalry. At his inauguration, Lincoln spoke directly to the former citizens of the South, reminding them that they were not enemies with the North, but friends. Still, within six weeks, the Fire-eaters (pro-slavery extremists who encouraged the separation of Southern states from the Union) answered Lincoln's call for peace with the bombardment of a federal installation in Charleston Harbor in South Carolina—Fort Sumter. Starting in the early morning hours of April 12, the fort was shelled for a day and a half, reduced to rubble, in order to keep Lincoln from sending supplies to the small number of federal troops garrisoned behind the fort's masonry walls. The Civil War had begun.

THE CALL OF HISTORY

In Richmond, Virginia's capital, a convention was called to discuss the issue of secession. Lee was gravely concerned about the future of his home state and of his country. A few days following the attack on Fort Sumter, Lee received a call to again meet with General Scott. Scott was so busy with the events of war that he was sleeping at night on a couch in his office.

Before sending the dispatch to Lee, Scott met with the U.S. secretary of state, William H. Seward. Scott had asked to resign in order to make way for a younger commander. The two men discussed possible replacements, all of whom were soldiers from the North, including George B. McClellan, Joseph Hooker, and William T. Sherman, but Scott would not hear of them. He had someone else in mind, as explained by Gene Smith, in his book *Lee and Grant*, "There is one officer who would make an excellent general," Scott said to Seward. "But I do not know whether we can rely upon him. He lives not far away, and I have sent over to see. If he comes in tomorrow, I shall know."

"I will not ask his name until you hear from him, then, General," Seward said. "Though I think I can guess whom you mean."

When Lee arrived on April 18, he first stopped by and shared a meal with one of his many cousins, Cassius Lee, along with his older brother, Smith, and another cousin, Samuel Phillips Lee. During dinner, Smith and Samuel, who were both in the U.S. Navy, talked about their future plans. Samuel vowed he would remain in his country's service, while Smith said he would follow Virginia if his home state seceded. The two cousins joked about attacking one another at sea and taking one another prisoner. Robert E. Lee sat through the family dinner saying very little.

From there, Lee continued along the streets of Washington, D.C., to the home of Francis Preston Blair, Samuel's father-in-law. Blair had summoned Lee to come to Washington to meet with him on the morning of April 18, before his meeting with General Scott.

Lee arrived at the Blair House, just across the street from the White House. Lee and Blair were soon sitting opposite one another, with Blair speaking vaguely at first, about war and Napoleon and a soldier's duty. Then, he spoke more plainly. With authorization from General Scott, Secretary of War Edwin M. Stanton, and even President Lincoln himself, he asked Lee if he would take command of the entire U.S. Army. Before the veteran soldier stood the offer of a lifetime.

Sins of the Father

Robert E. Lee's story begins with his father, Henry Lee III, the dashing figure of the Southern military man, one who formed himself out of the challenges of the American Revolutionary War and the politics that followed. A 1774 graduate of Princeton University, Lieutenant Colonel Henry Lee, also known as "Lighthorse Harry," was a true military hero. During the American Revolution, he was a cavalry officer and a great strategist—a swashbuckler, fiery, hotheaded, and a risk taker. When the British general Charles Cornwallis brought his beleaguered army from the Carolinas into Virginia, it was Henry's plan to bottle the British commander's forces in his home state while the French navy kept a British fleet at bay, giving General George Washington the opportunity to strike a death blow against the British and end the war. When Henry

Henry Lee III, also known as Lighthorse Harry, was a Revolutionary War hero who later served in the Continental Congress and was governor of Virginia. Lee died bankrupt and ostracized by his family on Cumberland Island, Georgia.

Lee said something, Washington and his subordinates paid close attention.

A DISSATISFIED LIFE

The War for Independence ended with Henry dissatisfied. He thought that the army had not advanced him far enough in rank. Now in his mid-twenties, Henry resigned the Continental army in 1782, a year after the battle of Yorktown. Henry married his nineteen-year-old cousin, Matilda Ludwell Lee, in April 1782. The marriage was a happy one, producing three children.

According to Clifford Dowdey's *Lee*, Henry had told the famed general Nathaniel Greene of his intentions "to make my way easy and comfortable." Henry became involved in get-rich-quick schemes, turning to land speculation. Unfortunately, he had little head for such business and soon spent what available funds he had, even needing to cover some of his debts by selling off the furthest corners of his Virginia lands. In 1788, he got involved in a canal building project with George Washington and fellow Virginian James Madison. He invested a significant amount of money only to have the project shelved. As his business ventures failed, Henry found himself in debt. His wife, Matilda, became so concerned he would sell off her land that she had a legal document drawn up placing her family lands in trust to their children.

In 1790, tragedy struck. After a lingering illness, Matilda died. Still in debt, Henry managed to convince the trustees of the property left to their children by Matilda to allow him to sell off several more acres to pay off his obligations.

From 1786–1788, Henry was a delegate to the Continental Congress. From 1789–1791, he served in the General Assembly, and in 1791, was elected governor of Virginia. That same year his oldest son died, which Henry took hard. Dowdey notes in his book *Lee* that Henry wrote to his friend Alexander Hamilton that the tragedy of losing his wife and his son "removed [him] far from the happy enjoyment of life."

With his family life less than satisfying, and often bored with his governorship, Henry went looking for another wife. He found a willing partner in Ann Hill Carter, and the couple married on a sultry Virginia day, June 18, 1793. A descendant of King Robert II of Scotland, Ann was from one of the wealthiest of Virginia's aristocratic families. His new wife was the heiress to 6,000 acres of fertile Virginia tobacco land on a grand estate called Shirley Plantation and owned dozens of slaves. The newlyweds lived in luxury in the estate house of Stratford Hall in Westmoreland County.

DOWNWARD TURN

The future seemed bright for Henry Lee. He had married well, and, everything indicated, so had she. Some spoke of him as a future president of the United States. Some of the Lees' brightest moments included the births of six more children, starting in 1795.

At the request of President George Washington, the former cavalry officer put his uniform back on to lead a militia unit of 15,000 against western Pennsylvania farmers who were violently protesting the new federal tax on whiskey producers. The appointment gained him a general's rank. Henry was still so well respected to many Americans that, when Washington died in 1799, he was tapped to deliver the eulogy. His words are still quoted today, "First in war, first in peace, first in the hearts of his countrymen."

Still, Henry's future would take a downward turn. Tobacco prices were falling, making profit for Virginia planters more elusive. Henry's debts mounted. He had gone through his first wife's fortune, and was on his way through his second wife's money. He sold off some of her ancestral lands and paintings out of the Great Hall. Henry gained the reputation as someone who did not pay his debts.

Henry was so deeply in debt that, according to Gene Smith's *Lee and Grant*, he "dodged down alleys in fear of creditors when he went to Alexandria or Richmond." Money became so tight at home that Ann did not have enough coal to heat the family home during the winter of 1806. She was pregnant again, with a child she did not relish having, as it would represent only one more mouth to feed. The boy was born on January 19, 1807, a difficult birth. She named him after her two brothers, Robert and Edward.

Stratford Hall plantation in Westmoreland County, Virginia, was the birthplace of Robert E. Lee and the home of four generations of the Lee family, including two signers of the Declaration of Independence. Today, the 1900 acres that make up the plantation along the Potomac River is a U.S. National Historic Landmark.

The Lees fortunes became so frightful that, when Robert E. Lee was only two years old, his father, who had once advised George Washington on military strategy and served his commonwealth home as governor, was tossed into debtor's prison, where he would remain for a year. During his incarceration, he tried to stay busy writing his memoirs of the great American War of Independence. He became convinced his book would become a best-seller, and was penning his words on paper he bought on credit.

For the Lees, these were the bleakest days. After losing their house to Henry's oldest son, they took residence in Alexandria where Ann rented a small house. Henry was no longer able to provide for his family, so Ann used the income from a small trust that paid $25 a week to support them. Henry spent his days telling his children stories of the war, wearing his old military cape around the streets of Alexandria.

A FUTILE ESCAPE

Things only went from bad to worse. On July 27, 1812, when young Robert was only five, his father was seriously injured while coming to the aid of a friend. Alexander Hanson, editor of the Baltimore newspaper *The Federal Republican*, was attacked by a Democratic-Republican mob for his editorials in opposition to the War of 1812. Henry and two dozen Federalists who had taken refuge in the offices of the paper were beaten for three hours. According to Gene Smith's *Lee and Grant*, "A drunk flung hot candle grease into Lee's eyes and then slashed at his face with a knife." The attack left Henry broken, his face badly scarred.

Just in his mid-50s, Henry was never well after the assault. His hair turned snowy white and his body was pale and thin. He longed for escape and for a warmer climate. Requesting help from President James Madison—who had served during the war with Henry—and Madison's secretary of state, James Monroe, Henry was given money to live in the West Indies.

From 1813–1818 he made Barbados his home, trying to recover his health, while writing biographies of President Washington and General Nathaniel Greene. His memoirs had been published as a two-volume set, but according to Clifford Dowdey's *Lee*, the work "won him neither the fame nor fortune for which he had wistfully hoped." He did write home to his family, mostly letters to his favorite son, Carter, who was attending Harvard and who rarely wrote his father back. As for Ann, she wrote little to her husband. In fact, she began referring to herself as the "Widow Lee." Henry's youngest children had only dim memories of their father.

By 1818, 62-year-old Henry Lee made the decision to return to Virginia and to his family. He never made it past Georgia. Falling ill, Henry requested the ship drop him off at Cumberland Island, off the coast of Georgia, at the estate of his old comrade-in-arms, Nathaniel Greene, who had died several years earlier. On March 25, 1818, he died and was buried with full military honors. No one in Henry's family attended the funeral, and Lighthorse Harry's burial plot went without a headstone for 15 years until one of his sons made the proper arrangements. It would be 44 years before any of Henry's children visited his grave site. The one who did was Robert E. Lee.

GROWING UP A LEADER

Henry's life would have a dramatic impact on his son, Robert Edward. It became a goal for Robert to live his life differently than his father, and his mother also worked hard to make certain of it. With Henry living in Barbados, her eldest son, Carter, at Harvard, and her middle son, Smith, a naval midshipman always at sea, Robert was the man of the house, even at age six. Ann came to rely heavily on her young son.

Young Robert was a good school student and was active in swimming, skating, and rowing. He looked after his family. Even before becoming a teenager, he was the one who went to market to buy food for the family and waited on his mother, seeing to her medications. He worked hard to become the man his father had never been—disciplined, devoted, loyal. According to Dowdey's *Lee*, before his death Henry saw these tendencies in his son even at an early age. One of the letters Henry wrote to his son Carter said, "Robert was always good and will be confirmed in his happy turn of mind by his ever-watchful and affectionate mother."

Despite these expectations, young Robert did find time for fun. He vacationed with some of his wealthier relatives. He was invited frequently to visit Stratford Hall, where he had been born. Before the scandal, the old mansion had become Henry Lee Jr.'s home, who, with money provided by his wealthy wife, had fixed the old place up. Robert went on fox hunts with relatives, even though there were times when he had no horse. He would run on foot, which helped turn him into a ramrod-straight young man with broad shoulders. In 1824, at age 17, Robert had the thrill of meeting the Marquis de Lafayette, the French aristocrat who had volunteered his services to then-General Washington during the Revolutionary War. Lafayette, while visiting Alexandria, Virginia, requested a visit to the widow of his former comrade, Lighthorse Harry Lee. Ann hosted the old Frenchman in her parlor, with Robert at her side.

As Robert came of age, he wondered where he could possibly go in life, with little money available. Although his older brother Carter had gone to Harvard, Carter wasted much of his opportunity, spending money the family did not have and wasting time drinking heavily with friends. There was no money for Robert to go to college, even though he considered becoming a doctor. Then, he gave thought to the military. The United States Military Academy at West Point would require no money, and his Virginia family certainly had connections. In 1825, Robert was accepted to West Point.

The day Robert left for West Point was a sad one for all. Ann had already sent two of her sons out into the world and Robert would be her third. Yet his mother's sense of loss for her son was overwhelming. To a cousin, Ann confided, according to historian Emory Thomas, "How can I live without Robert? He is both son and daughter to me."

A SOLDIER IN THE MAKING

A year after her son left home, Ann Lee remarried, to William Louis Marshall from Baltimore. While she was never in good health again, she enjoyed frequent visits from her children. Although Robert was not able to come home often, she was kept informed of his success at West Point through various family members.

Between 1824–1825, during the year between Robert's acceptance and his first year at West Point, he used his time to prepare for the rigors of the academy. A neighbor, a Quaker named James Hallowell, had opened a school next door to the Lees and Robert signed up for study. Hallowell was soon impressed with the 18-year-old, as noted by author Clifford Dowdey:

> His specialty was *finishing up*. He imparted a finish and a neatness, as he proceeded, to everything he undertook. One of the branches of mathematics he studied was Conic Sections, in which some of the diagrams are very complicated. He drew the diagrams on a slate; and although he well knew that the one he was drawing would have to be removed to make room for another, he drew each one with as much accuracy and finish, lettering and all, as if it were to be engraved and printed.

Hallowell also noted that young Robert appeared, to him, to have fully developed his personality and character, even at age 18, even before leaving home for military school.

TO THE ACADEMY

Established in 1802 by Thomas Jefferson, West Point is situated on the high bluffs overlooking the Hudson River in New York State. In 1825, Robert's freshman year, it was a simple complex of four grayish, stone buildings scattered across an open plain. A pair of the buildings were barracks, the third a mess hall, and the fourth the true seat of learning, where 200 young cadets studied in the two-story structure that served as classrooms, the academy library, a laboratory, and the chapel. Those who were accepted to the academy worked through a four-year program that included studies in military organization, the strictures of marching, battlefield tactics and formations, and the established principles of war, some dating back thousands of years. This being the nineteenth century, cadets were also introduced to the latest designs for military architecture: how to build temporary bridges and how to structure canals and forts. Although still a young institution, West Point had been established with a sense of purpose—to instill discipline in those who would lead America's troops, as well as form true character—and it was already the best military academy and engineering school in the United States.

In 1825, Lee began his military training and became an exemplary student; in fact, he was the best in the military academy's history, then and now. He excelled in every way—in his studies, his decorum, his spit and polish. He applied himself constantly and consistently, placing himself in the top five of his class of distinguished cadets. He adapted quickly to the routine and rigors of West Point and applied all the discipline that had been drilled into him under his mother's watch and care that it was practically second nature. By the end of his freshman year, he was given the most prestigious honor of his class, an appointment as staff sergeant, the highest noncommissioned rank of the fourth classmen, or freshmen.

Among the records Lee achieved for himself at West Point, perhaps none was more impressive than his spotless cadet record. Through his years at the academy, he never accumulated a single demerit, a distinction he shared with only five other cadets in the history of the academy. Smith's *Lee and Grant* describes Lee's success: "His buttons gleamed. His sword was spotless. He was never late for formation, never had his bed made up in less than perfect fashion, was never guilty of a sloppy salute, missed no bed checks, was not cited for abusing a horse or for folding his towel incorrectly."

By Lee's second year at the academy, he not only excelled in his studies, he was asked to serve as acting assistant professor of mathematics, tutoring math-challenged freshmen. He was paid $10 for this special duty, which gave his mother Ann an additional sense of pride in her son. At year's end, he finally made a trip back home to Virginia. He had been gone for two years. Robert E. Lee was now 20, looking splendid in his cadet gray uniform, and in the best of health. He enjoyed the summer with family, including his many cousins.

His final two years of study at West Point were focused on the subject he wanted to pursue as a military man—engineering. He took science courses and learned the arts of field and permanent fortifications. Engineering was typically pursued by the most serious students, and Lee saw it as a field that could prepare him for a life's profession, in or out of the military. His senior year, Robert was the school's top cadet, and he was honored with yet another prestigious appointment, this time as corps adjutant, the highest rank a cadet could achieve. Not only had Lee managed through his years as a cadet to win the approval and favor of the school's officials, but he was recognized by his fellow cadets as a man of honor and dignity. In *Lee*, Clifford Dowdey cites West Point classmate and Civil War general Joseph Johnston's observations of the unparalleled merits of Cadet Lee:

> We had the same intimate associates, who thought as I did, that no other youth or man so united the qualities that win warm friendship and command high respect. For he was full of sympathy and kindness, genial and fond of gay conversation, even fun, while his correctness of demeanor and attention to all duties, personal and official, and dignity as much a part of himself as the elegance of his person, gave him a superiority that every one acknowledged in his heart.

In June 1829, after four years of study, Brevet Second Lieutenant Robert E. Lee graduated from West Point second in his class of 46 and head of the class in artillery and tactics. There was no family celebration, however, for his mother was dying. He went home and witnessed her last days. According to Dowdey, "It was told that her dark eyes followed him whenever he left the

room, and her gaze remained on the door until he came back in."
He was at her side when her spirit finally left her in July.

Upon Lee's graduation from the academy, he was accepted
into the ranks of the Corps of Engineers, an elite unit in the
U.S. military. The engineers were responsible for building and
maintaining military installations including forts and coastal
facilities, but also worked closely with other federal government entities on such internal improvements as roads, bridges,
and flood control. Over the next two years, he worked on
coastal fortifications in Georgia and Virginia, then north to
New York, where he did survey work to clear up state boundary
disputes. He took along the slave who had served his mother so
loyally for so many years, Nat. He did his work well, but it did
not gain him much attention from superiors.

A NEW BRIDE

In 1831, two years following his mother's death, Robert found
himself a bride. Mary Anna Randolph Custis was the great-
granddaughter of Martha Washington by her first husband,
Daniel Parke Custis, and step-great-granddaughter of George
Washington. As the only child of George Custis (who was
adopted by George Washington) to survive into adulthood,
young Mary had inherited Arlington House, where the Marquis de Lafayette had stayed during his 1824 visit, as well as two
additional estates, one along the James River peninsula, called
White House, and another named Romancoke. Modeled after
a Greek temple, the Arlington estate sat on a high hill looking
east toward Washington, D.C., and included 15,000 acres and
250 slaves.

Mary Custis was a delicate blond who was well read and
perhaps a bit spoiled. She was forgetful, despised habit and
routine, and was capable of fits of temper. Despite this, Lee
was interested and began writing letters to her. While he was
charming, he was still a military man with no money, court-
ing a young woman of substance. It was not surprising that

Mary's father was less than enthusiastic when Lee came calling. Nevertheless, Lee had a reputation as an intelligent and thoughtful young man, qualities that Mary's mother noticed. Although her husband protested, Mrs. Custis did not have significant oppositions to Lieutenant Lee. The two young people

LEE'S VIEWS ON SLAVERY

While Virginia was one of the largest of the slaveholding states during the decades leading up to the Civil War, some Southerners did not support the institution, if not in reality, then at least in spirit. One of those was Robert E. Lee. Although he had been raised with slaves all around him, as an adult Lee came to feel that slavery was wrong. According to Stanley F. Horn's *Robert E. Lee Reader*, Lee wrote a letter to his wife in late 1856 in which he stated: "In this enlightened age there are few, I believe, but what will acknowledge that slavery, as an institution, is a moral and political evil."

Lee had come to this conclusion after nearly 50 years of living in the South. It is unlikely he had much direct contact with the working conditions of field workers. More commonly, he experienced slavery through relationships with his closest neighbors, the vast majority of whom treated their slaves fairly well. Given his limited exposure to the institution, Lee supported gradual emancipation, although he still regarded blacks as inferior to whites. In the letter to Mary he stated his views on emancipation and his preferred general timetable: "The blacks are immeasurably better off here than in Africa, morally, socially, and physically. The painful discipline they are undergoing is necessary for their instruction as a race and, I hope, will prepare and lead them to better things. . .."

began seeing one another and the relationship intensified quickly, as quoted in Smith's *Lee and Grant*:

> When Mrs. Custis remarked that Robert had been read-
> ing aloud from Sir Walter Scott for quite a time and was

In actuality, Lee supported gradual emancipation for economic reasons. While not an expert in economics, the lifelong agrarian did not feel the institution of slavery—which created a workforce that existed from cradle to grave—was very efficient.

He did not like abolitionists, however, considering them outsiders who tried to push their political agenda on others. He described abolitionists, as presented in Thomas Emory's book, *Robert E. Lee: A Biography*, as "certain people of the North" who were trying to "interfere with & change the domestic institutions of the South. . . . Their object is both unlawful & entirely foreign." Lee went on to predict, with great and unfortunate accuracy, that the abolitionists would achieve their ultimate goals "through the agency of a civil & servile war."

Lee opposed the institution of slavery, even as he opposed the tactics and rhetoric of the abolitionists. Yet, he had no clear answers concerning how the institution could be effectively ended. He believed that when the time came for slavery to end in America, God would bring about its destruction. Lee wrote: "How long their subjugation may be necessary is known & ordered by a wise Merciful Providence. Their emancipation will sooner result from the mild & melting influence of Christianity, then [from] the storm and tempests of fiery Controversy."

Mary Custis Lee had an illustrious pedigree. She was the step-great granddaughter of George Washington and her father, George Washington Parke Custis, was one of the most prominent residents in Alexandria County, Virginia. Her father hosted many famous men at Arlington, the family home, including the Marquis de Lafayette.

perhaps tired and hungry, and that perhaps Mary ought to take him into the dining room where there was some fruitcake on a sideboard. When they came out it was announced they were engaged.

The couple married in the family drawing room of Arlington House on June 30, 1831. The whole affair was quite elaborate. Mary had six bridesmaids and the 3rd U.S. Artillery served as honor guard. After the wedding the couple enjoyed several weeks of Virginia festivities including banquets, dances, and fox hunts. In August 1831, Robert's leave was up and the newlyweds soon took residence in the officers' quarters at Fort Monroe on the eastern tip of the Virginia peninsula, between the York and the James rivers. It was a step down in living conditions for the genteel aristocratic daughter, but she had married a soldier. She was allowed to bring along a pair of slaves to serve as house servants.

SEPARATED BY DUTY

The army continued to provide a good fit for Lee, who was now 24 years. He had good friends among the other officers, enjoyed attending the local horse races and time spent with his academy chum, Joseph Johnston, who, like Lee, could enjoy an evening without alcohol, save the occasional glass of wine. He was still an easy man to associate with and appreciated by fellow officers and enlisted men alike. He was also extremely popular with the wives of the post officers. Both men and women took notice of him, especially his poise and demeanor. According to Douglas Southall Freeman's *Lee of Virginia*, one Lee observer at the post recalled how "my eye fell upon his face in perfect repose and the thought at once flashed through my mind: 'you certainly look more like a great man than anyone I have ever seen.'"

Mary, on the other hand, did not relish being an army officer's wife. Their living quarters were cramped and life at the post bored her. She did not make friends easily since she did not enjoy chitchat with other people, and there were no women at the post with whom she particularly liked spending much time.

When Lee and his wife went home to visit with her family during the holidays, she asked him to return to the post without her. But even as he departed from her at the first of the new year, in 1832, Mary was already pregnant. Later that year, Mary returned to the post to be with her husband and their son, George Washington Custis Lee, arrived that September, born on the second floor of Building No. 17 at the fort. During Christmas 1832, with a baby in her arms, she asked again to stay in Arlington. Throughout much of the time Lee was posted at Fort Monroe he was separated from Mary. Still, six other children were born over the next 13 years including Mary (1835); William Henry Fitzhugh (1837), whom the family always called "Rooney"; Ann (1839); Agnes (1841); Robert Edward Jr. (1843); and Mildred (1845). Of Lee's four daughters, none ever married.

From 1834–1837, Lee served as the assistant to Brigadier General Charles Gratiot, chief engineer in Washington D.C. In 1837, he was dispatched out to St. Louis. His immediate task was to apply his engineering skills to bring improvements to the various Mississippi River channels. His work took three years and was elemental in keeping the river flowing along the docks of the Missouri city. Lee was tireless in his efforts, as noted by the city's mayor. His hard work paid off in 1838 when he received a captain's rank. According to Douglas Southall Freeman's *R. E. Lee*, May John Darby observed how Lee

> went in person with the hands every morning about sunrise, and worked day by day in the hot, broiling sun. . . . He shared in the hard task and common fare and rations furnished to the common laborers . . . He maintained and preserved under all circumstances his dignity and gentlemanly bearing, winning and commanding the esteem, regard, and respect of every one under him.

By 1841, he was off to another assignment, this one at Fort Hamilton in New York, named for Alexander Hamilton. There he

Winfield Scott served on active duty as general longer than any other man in history. Over his 50-year-military career, Scott commanded forces in several wars and created the Union strategy known as the Anaconda Plan, which was used to defeat the Confederacy during the Civil War.

remained stationed for five years, working on the harbor defenses along the fort, and other works at Fort Lafayette in Brooklyn, and Battery Hudson and Battery Morton on Staten Island.

During the latter stages of his work in and around New York City, Lee received another appointment to West Point. This time, however, he was to serve on the Board of Visitors of the academy, which scrutinized the senior cadets as they neared graduation. The appointment began in the summer of 1844, and it put Lee in almost daily contact with General Winfield Scott, whom he came to admire and to whom he remained extremely loyal. Scott, then 58 years old, was a fellow Virginian who had received his captain's commission directly from President Thomas Jefferson. He emerged from the War of 1812 as a hero and been considered the previous year as a possible presidential candidate for the Whig Party. At six feet five inches, Scott was a large, impressive man whom Lee would come to know well in the years ahead.

During the short time the two men worked together on the West Point board, Scott became quite impressed with the junior officer. By 1846, Lee had 17 years of military service behind him, plus his four years of training at West Point. The year would prove crucial to the next phase of Lee's military career as it would be for many other U.S. Army officers. That year Scott called Lee to accompany him into a new area of service. In 1846, the United States and Mexico were going to war.

"The Best Soldier in Christendom"

The war between the United States and Mexico that began in 1846 did not represent the first time Mexicans and Americans had fought one another in recent years. During the 1830s, Mexican dictator Antonio Lopez de Santa Anna had tried to close off the northern Mexican province of Tejas (present-day Texas) from additional American colonization and encouraged the Mexican Congress to pass laws that restricted life for American settlers. Thousands of Americans who had moved to Tejas had rebelled against the Mexican government. Several provinces formed their own governments and the Texians declared their independence from Mexico. Santa Anna attacked the Zacatecan militia, the largest and best supplied forces in Mexico. After two hours of combat, Santa Anna's army defeated the militia, and Santa Anna made plans to defeat the Texians.

FROM REVOLUTION TO WAR

Unrest followed throughout Mexico and war began in Texas on October 2, 1835. Early Texian successes were followed by crushing defeat. Although the Texians experienced massive loss of lives, the Texas War of Independence led to the creation of the Republic of Texas. The Texas Revolution also created a new problem regarding the border between Texas and Mexico.

The dispute continued into the 1840s as Texas was finally annexed as an American state in 1845. Mexico continued to claim ownership of Texas and refused to recognize the military victory in 1836. The border issue soon became a clash between Mexico and the American government. President James K. Polk sent troops to the northern banks of the Rio Grande, the river he claimed was the appropriate border of Texas. This angered the Mexican government, which claimed that the Nueces River (about 150 miles north of the Rio Grande) as its border with Texas. The Mexican government declared that Polk was placing American forces on Mexican territory. When the Mexican government dispatched troops to remove the Americans, Polk had managed exactly what he had intended: He had baited the Mexican government to attack U.S. forces, giving him the opportunity to call for a declaration of war by the U.S. Congress.

As for 39-year-old Robert E. Lee, he was not enthusiastic about the conflict and how it had begun. According to Gene Smith, Lee expressed dismay: "We have bullied [Mexico]. For that I am ashamed." But he was soon on his way to Mexico. He was assigned in August 1846 as an assistant engineer of a unit of American forces under the command of General John E. Wool. By the time Lee reached Wool's camp in San Antonio in September, the war was nearly four months old. With war ahead of him, Lee had made out his will, leaving what little he had to his wife, Mary, with the estate to be distributed to his children upon her death.

Lee's military skills would not be needed until his unit began to move into Mexican territory. Until then, Lee taught troops how to build temporary bridges and repair roads. The Virginian began to fear the war would be over before he saw any action. By the beginning of 1847, however, he was on the move. He wrote a letter to his wife on January 17, informing her he had been called by General Scott to report to general headquarters along the Brazos in Texas.

When he arrived, Lee became part of an engineering corps that included the military men who would one day be among the most important officers who fought in the Civil War. First Lieutenant Pierre Gustave Toutant Beauregard from Louisiana would serve under Lee during the Civil War, as well as Pennsylvanian George B. McClellan, a recent graduate of West Point, against whom Lee would fight on more than one occasion, including the Battle of Antietam. Lee's friend and former classmate Joseph Johnston was assigned to the topographical engineers with George Gordon Meade, who would one day defeat Lee at Gettysburg. But in 1847, the Civil War still lay off in the distance.

Most important to Lee, however, was that he was once again at the side of Major General Winfield Scott. In short order, Scott brought Lee into his inner circle of staff officers, an important group that Scott referred to as his "little cabinet." Together they discussed Scott's strategy. With American naval vessels blockading the coast, army forces would be landing at Veracruz, Mexico's most important port. His men would then capture the city, hopefully resulting in the surrender of the Mexican government, given the loss of such a strategic port. If the Mexicans did not surrender, Scott planned to lead his forces into the heart of Mexico, marching over the 200 miles that separated Veracruz from the Mexican capital, Mexico City. Capturing Mexico City was certain to bring about an immediate end to the war.

HEROIC DUTY

By March 9, Lee began to see the action he had been afraid to miss. That day, U.S. forces began their first large-scale amphibious assault, hitting the Caribbean beaches just south of Veracruz. A week later, Scott dispatched Lee and Johnston ashore to scout out potential positions for American artillery to be set up, which was a duty of the engineer corps.

After Lee and Johnston completed their reconnaissance, they made their way back to camp. Along the way, while passing through some brush along a narrow trail, they stumbled upon a U.S. sentry. A highly excitable sentinel fired point-blank at Lee. The musket ball barely missed Lee, ripping his coat. Had the wild shot been a fraction of an inch to the left, Lee would have been killed. Lee requested that the incident be overlooked, but General Scott ordered that the young soldier be punished.

During the days that followed the amphibious landing near Veracruz, Lee was assigned the task of establishing gun positions that would ultimately ring the city in a semicircle. By March 24, the bombardment of the port town commenced with Lee personally commanding an artillery unit. The enemy responded, and shot and shell was soon pouring down in the vicinity of Lee's position. It was the first time the 39-year-old soldier had been under direct fire. In his letters home from these days, he gives no indication he had any concern for his personal safety, just for the safety of his brother Smith, who was in command of a shipboard battery. On March 29, the city of Veracruz surrendered.

Following the March landing and capture of Veracruz, Scott's army began a methodical campaign inland toward Mexico City that lasted six months. During that time, Lee was busy applying his engineering skills to the military landscape. General Santa Anna was no longer the Mexican president, but he longed to return to executive power again. Santa Anna ordered the Mexican army to protect a narrow pass called *Cerro Gordo* (Fat Hill), that included a difficult set of landforms with

In order to advance inland during the Mexican-American War, American forces, led by General Winfield Scott, needed to conquer Veracruz, the strongest fortress in the Americas at the time. On March 9, 1847, the first large-scale amphibious assault conducted by U.S. forces was a success, and, after 20 days of fighting, the Battle of Veracruz ended with the surrender and occupation of the city.

mountain ridges and a line of conic-shaped hills, which established a natural barrier that extended across a level meadow called *Plan del Rio* (the River Plain). With a force of 12,000 men, Santa Anna blocked the path of 10,000 U.S. forces. There was little option but to determine a means to bypass the enemy. General Scott gave the task to Lee, sending his engineer to figure out a way by which the American commander could move his men by the left flank to a position beyond Cerro Gordo.

Lee had to secretly move in close to the enemy, sometimes having to crawl on the ground among thickets of desert scrub, just to see the positions of the Mexican forces. At one point, he crawled up on a local spring where the Mexicans filled their canteens daily. As he lay quietly on the ground, a group of Mexican soldiers approached the creek. Lee managed to crawl behind a fallen log where he remained hidden throughout the rest of the day, with soldiers sometimes sitting on the log just a few feet away. The day was blisteringly hot and mosquitoes buzzed around Lee constantly, but he managed to remain undetected until nightfall. Finally, he took the opportunity to crawl away and report back to an anxious General Scott. By the time of his return, he had been gone for so long that his name was among those officially missing.

Lee's reconnaissance report gave Scott the information he needed to make the decision to move by his left, cut off the Mexicans' lines of communication and dislodge the enemy from their earthen fortifications. Lee told Scott of a location along the ridge where cannon might be hauled up, but it would require the use of ropes along cliff ledges and the help of surefooted mules. The following day, April 16, Lee returned to the place where he hid the previous day, with a small band of soldiers. They cut their way through the local thickets and opened a route for a large group to advance around Cerro Gordo so they could reach a site behind the Mexican army's main encampment. With sheer determination, Lee and his men managed to haul artillery pieces straight up along the cliff sides.

On April 17, Scott's forces attacked Santa Anna's men. Trying to cover ground that was extremely uneven and scattered with large rocks and dry arroyos (brooks), Lee and those following his lead came under fire. Lee kept his cool, giving direction to artillery units and soon American cannon were hitting targets along the Mexican lines. With American troops approaching him from more than one direction and threatening his line of retreat, General Santa Anna ordered his men to fall back before they could be captured *en masse*. Hurriedly, the Mexican commander hightailed himself to safety on the back of a mule. Lee's first battle ended with an American win and much of the success of the day was due to his organized flanking measures.

Lee was immediately hailed as the hero of the American actions in and around Cerro Gordo. His exploits would result in Lee receiving a brevet major advancement in rank within a few months of the campaign. On the evening of April 18, after Lee had spent days crawling around in bug-infested ravines and had labored with heavy cannon up cliff walls, he was in residence at the Haciendo Encero, a well-appointed, comfortable Mexican villa. In a letter he wrote to Mary back at Arlington, he did not fret for himself, but for his brother in arms, Joseph Johnston, who had been seriously wounded in both an arm and his hip.

ON TO MEXICO CITY

After a few weeks in the local town of Jalapa, on May 15 Scott's army was once again on the move, this time to Puebla, the second largest city in Mexico. Scott's advance was interrupted when he received orders to give up some of his men who were needed north to augment another U.S. military force, this one under the command of General Zachary Taylor. For three months, they remained in Puebla. Not one to sit still for long, Lee spent much of his time mapping the region. Finally, tired of waiting, General Scott made a bold decision. On August 7, after receiving significant reinforcements and deciding to abandon his supply lines, he ordered his men to move forward and resume their march toward Mexico City. Forward he moved with 11,000 soldiers, including some cavalry.

Scott's army made progress toward Mexico City and, within four days, the Americans reached a long rise at the 10,000-foot elevation. Before them was the great high valley of central Mexico. Still, ahead lay difficult terrain, covered with lakes and marshes, where the army could only move safely along man-made roads. Again Captain Lee and his engineers were dispatched to find the most reasonable approach for Scott's forces to advance toward Mexico City. Reporting back, Lee and his colleagues suggested the army move around the south end of Lake Xochimilco, which lay southeast of the Mexican capital.

On August 18, Scott's forces reached San Augustin. The Mexican capital lay only ten miles in the distance. Nonetheless, those final ten miles represented an extraordinarily difficult terrain for the American forces. It was a region known as the *pedregal*, a vast no-man's-land lava bed that lay like a rock-strewn, agitated sea frozen in time. Only two roads passed across the eerie landscape, and the Mexican army had them heavily fortified. On August 19, General Scott sent Lee into the region, this time along with 500 men, following a forgotten wagon trail. At one point, Lee and his colleagues came under rifle fire from a group of Mexican soldiers. When the Americans returned fire, the Mexicans backed off.

The American detachment crossed the lava bed with some difficulty, then cut through a stronghold of brush thickets until they reached a point Lee thought good for cannon placement. Lee and his men then recrossed the *pedregal* that night during a heavy deluge. Only brilliant flashes of lightning kept them on course, giving an occasional view of the landscape where they needed to go next. Lee's efforts that night would gain the further respect of General Scott who, according to Freeman's *R. E. Lee*, referred to Lee's daring as "the greatest feat of physical and moral courage" of the entire war. Once again, through Lee's engineering skills and his courage, the American army flanked the Mexicans, and the capital appeared within their grasp.

The final battle for Mexico City came a few weeks later on September 13, during the largest scale engagement of the conflict, the battle at Chapultepec, a large stone fortification guarding the eastern approach to the capital. For two straight days, Lee did not sleep, as the fight raged on. At one point he received a wound, his second. Close to victory, General Scott sent Lee to the front with a message for General William Worth. Lee delivered the message on horseback, then returned to the rear and reported to Scott, only to fall from his horse due to loss of blood from his wound and absolute exhaustion.

Although U.S. forces had managed to drive the Mexican army guarding Mexico City from their positions in the west, General Scott and his council were interested in attacking from the south against Chapultepec. Chapultepec Castle, a former Mexican military academy, was an important position for the defense of the city. Young officers during the Mexican-American War, Lee and Ulysses S. Grant would lead armies on opposite sides during the Civil War.

With the occupation of Mexico City, the war was over and Lee's commanding officer and mentor was the hero of the day. But there was also lavish praise for Lee. Lieutenant Richard Ewell, who would command troops under Lee at Gettysburg, wrote to his brother, as described in James Robertson's book, *Robert E. Lee*: "I really think one of the most talented men connected with this army is Captain Lee, of the Engineers. By his daring reconnaissance pushed up to the cannon's mouth, he has enabled General Scott to fight his battles almost without leaving his tent." As Gene Smith writes, Scott himself would refer to Captain Robert E. Lee as "The best soldier in Christendom . . . Without whose aid we should not be here now."

This was Lee's first taste of war, one that delivered beyond the classroom lessons of West Point's maps and books. It was real combat, harrowing and life threatening. Perhaps the most important lesson for Lee was that a smaller force, if led properly, may well defeat an enemy that numbers many more. The value of flanking maneuvers, of fortified earthworks, of cutting communication lines when necessary, good reconnaissance and accurate intelligence, and an aggressive audacity—these were the other studies Lee was able to glean from in the war. He also learned hard lessons, those of sacrifice and death. It would motivate him during the war to write a letter to his son, Custis, according to historian J. William Jones, in which he made a grim and sober note: "You have no idea what a horrible sight a battlefield is."

DAYS OF WANDERING

The United States emerged from war with Mexico with vast landholdings as its reward. The Treaty of Guadalupe Hidalgo, signed on February 2, 1848, by American diplomat Nicholas Trist, gave the United States undisputed claim to Texas, established the U.S.-Mexico border at the Rio Grande, and ceded to the United States the present-day states of California, Nevada, Utah, New Mexico, Arizona, and parts of Colorado and Wyoming.

Lee had gone to Mexico as a captain and returned a colonel, even if brevet, or temporary. He had gone to Mexico a well-trained military engineer and returned a heroic veteran of war. By the time he returned to his family in Arlington, he had been gone for two years. He did not even recognize his youngest son, Robert Jr., who was nicknamed "Bertus." At the family reunion, the returning war hero hugged a neighbor's child, thinking he was Bertus.

Lee was assigned work that kept him closer to home. He inspected the coastal defenses in Florida and, by April 1849, was in Baltimore, in charge of the construction of Fort Carroll along the Patapsco River. Forty-five years old with children between the ages of 17 and 4, Lee was happy to be home. His son Robert Jr. recalled these days in his book, *Recollections and Letters of General Robert E. Lee*, published in 1904:

> At forty-five years of age he was active, strong and as handsome as he had ever been . . . He was always bright and gay with us little folk, romping, playing and joking with us . . . Although he was so joyous and familiar with us, he was very firm on all proper occasions, never indulged us in anything that was not good for us, and exacted the most implicit obedience. I always knew that it was impossible to disobey my father.

In 1852, an enviable command was handed Lee, which made up for the dreary work at Baltimore—appointment as superintendent of the United States Military Academy at West Point. He had been in the military for 23 years by then; the academy offered him not only a prestigious command, but also it allowed him to be constantly in the company of his family. He moved his family to the academy in August.

HALCYON DAYS

Lee's assignment at West Point was an important stepping stone in his military career, but the Virginian longed for something more. By 1855, another opportunity came his way. That year, the U.S. Army added, with congressional approval, two new infantry regiments and two cavalry. Lee needed a change, and the cavalry looked like the way for Lee to go. General Scott and Secretary of War Jefferson Davis, who would later be elected president of the Confederacy during the Civil War, offered Lee an assignment with the newly formed 2nd U.S. Cavalry, although they disagreed on whether Lee should lead the unit. Scott supported Lee, while Davis threw his support behind one of his closest military associates, Colonel Albert Sidney Johnston. Ultimately, Secretary Davis had his way, and Johnston became the cavalry unit's commander, with Lee appointed as his second in command. The payoff for Lee was immediate. His new assignment came with a new rank, a double promotion to lieutenant colonel. His brevet status was no more.

WEST WITH THE CAVALRY

Lee's new duties would soon separate him from his family once again. In March 1855, Lee left for Louisville, Kentucky, where the 2nd Cavalry was being established. The 2nd Cavalry could not have asked for better commanders in Johnston and Lee. Once the 2nd was largely formed (they would still be adding recruits even later), Johnston, Lee, and their men left Louisville to take up duty in the frontier region of Texas, to Camp Cooper. After three years in the arms of his family at West Point, Lee was now 1,800 miles away from them.

Texas turned out to be a miserable assignment for Lee. This remote outpost where American Indians still lived was home to 12 officers and 26 enlisted men, living on a bleak, dry plain where the local water supply was always muddy, and the landscape was a desert of scattered cactus and chaparral stands. Lee, always an avid gardener, could not get vegetables to grow properly. He missed his family dearly and wrote home as he found the time, in between giving chase to bands of marauding American Indians who harassed wagon roads and remote settlements.

After a year and a half in Texas, Johnston was summoned to an assignment in Washington, and Lee became the regiment's commander. The advancement meant a move to San Antonio. Two months later, in October 1857, Mary's father died and Lee went to Arlington to comfort the family. He had not seen his wife in close to two years, and was shocked to find that her health had deteriorated so severely she was disabled. Besides tending to Mary, Lee carried out his role as executor of Mary's father's will. Mary inherited the Arlington properties and the large house. Upon his return, Lee found Arlington in a state of disrepair and the estate deep in a pile of leftover debts. Fences were down, the roof of the mansion leaked, the yard had gone to seed, and George Custis's will called for his nearly 200 slaves to be freed within five years of his death.

With everything in such a poor state of affairs, Lee applied for leave from the army and remained at Arlington for the next two years. Through this time, he struggled to repair the damage of years of neglect Custis had brought to Arlington and the other land holdings. He rented out Custis's slaves to other plantations, since he did not need nearly all of them to do work for him. These two years were frustrating for Lee. He had left his military career behind, even if temporarily, and his work at Arlington kept him busy with mundane, difficult labors that required no special skills.

Then, on October 17, 1859, Lee was told to report to Secretary of War John B. Floyd. Abolitionists, under the leadership of the fiery John Brown, had attacked the federal arsenal at Harpers Ferry, Virginia, in an attempt to invoke a slave rebellion.

THE RAID ON HARPERS FERRY

By 1859, the country was in turmoil over what had become the most important and emotional political issue of the nineteenth century—the expansion of slavery into the western territories of the United States. The Missouri Compromise of 1820 had allowed Missouri to enter the Union as a new slave state, while closing off slavery from the northern reaches of the old Louisiana Purchase territory.

Later, events complicated and even resurrected the slavery expansion issue. With the territory gained from Mexico following the Mexican-American War, the issue of expanding the slave states further west was back on the table. Then, in 1850, the territory of California, prompted by the increase in population due to the gold rush of 1849, applied for statehood as a free state. While Congress agreed, a series of bills called the Compromise of 1850 had opened up the remainder of the lands gained from the Mexican-American War. These measures were meant to balance the power between the free states and the slave states. The laws did not include the Wilmot Proviso, which would have banned slavery in the territory acquired from Mexico.

The Kansas-Nebraska Act of 1854, designed by Illinois senator Stephen A. Douglas, created the territories of Kansas and Nebraska. Power was left in the hands of the people in those territories to determine whether they wanted slavery or not by taking a vote. Despite the Missouri Compromise of three decades earlier, the new Kansas and Nebraska territories were now thrown open to the possibility of slavery being established there. During the years that followed, anti-slavery advocates and pro-slavery supporters moved out to Kansas and intimidated others to join their separate causes.

Slave politics quickly devolved into bloodshed, as Border Ruffians (slavery supporters) killed abolitionists and vice versa. Among those who had gone out to Kansas to engage in the bloody conflict, which became known as "Bleeding Kansas," was the gray-bearded, wild-eyed John Brown. Brown and several of his sons had engaged in raids against pro-slavery settlements in Kansas and killed several men. During one raid at Pottawatomie Creek, Brown and his followers had pulled five pro-slavery men out of their cabins at night and hacked them to death with broadswords, leaving their entrails scattered across the dark Kansas earth.

Things boiled to a head in 1857 after the U.S. Supreme Court handed down one of the most significant decisions made by the nation's highest court during the nineteenth century. In *Dred Scott v. Sandford*, the court had ruled against Dred Scott, a black man who had sued for his freedom on the grounds that

While Lee served as superintendent of West Point, James Elwell Brown Stuart, also known as Jeb, was a student. When he graduated in 1854, Jeb was one of eight cadets designated an honorary cavalry officer and was a friend of the Lee family. During the Civil War, Jeb served as a cavalry commander and Lee depended on Jeb as his eyes and ears.

he had been taken by his owner into the free state of Illinois and into free territories to live for several years. The court not only decided against Scott, but declared that he, as a black man, had no rights that any white man had to respect. The Courts also stated that the federal government had no power to limit where slavery should or should not exist, which opened up all territories to the potential of legal slavery.

An angry John Brown, in part motivated by the *Dred Scott* decision, had decided to act. As slavery now had the opportunity to spread without limit, perhaps even into free states themselves, he was convinced the institution must be destroyed. He and a handful of followers had organized a plan for a raid on the federal arsenal at Harpers Ferry, Virginia, (today in West Virginia) where the conspirators could gain access to thousands of muskets which could be used to arm the slaves. This, he hoped, would lead to a slave uprising that Brown, in his wildest imaginations, believed might spread across the South, involving hundreds of thousands of slaves and resulting in the violent end of the institution he had hated since he was a young man.

On October 16, 1859, Brown and his men managed to capture the arsenal, but also killed a free black man, the town's railroad station baggage master. The townspeople, alerted by warning bells in nearby Charles Town, angrily turned on the invaders as Brown and his followers took hostages and holed up in the town's engine house. Two of Brown's men had been captured and another two killed. With a local railroad running into Harpers Ferry, word was sent out by telegraph to Washington concerning the raid. When the message reached the War Department, James Elwell Brown Stuart, also known as Jeb, a veteran of several American Indian conflicts, happened to be there. He was to present a new device he had created for attaching a cavalry officer's saber scabbard to his belt. He was quickly sent across the Potomac to deliver word to Lee that he was needed.

ENDING THE SIEGE

Wearing civilian clothes, Lee did not take time to change into a uniform, but left instantly with Stuart. Soon, they were meeting with the secretary of war and President James Buchanan. By five that afternoon, both Lee and Stuart boarded a train on the Baltimore & Ohio Railroad, headed to the U.S. Arsenal, where they arrived by 10 P.M. Once on the scene, Lee was informed that approximately 20 white men were inside the engine house, having been driven there by a unit of Virginia militia. One of their hostages was a relative of Lee's, the aged Colonel Lewis Washington, grandnephew of George Washington. The other hostages included several arsenal workers, a local farmer, and a half dozen of the farmer's slaves.

Lee's task was daunting. Dozens of people were in the engine house, captors and captives all mixed together, barricaded in. The engine house itself was a stronghold, a stone building measuring 35 feet across with large, stone-supported, double oak doors. Although the insurrectionists were contained and the slave uprising never materialized, his immediate goal was to free the hostages and to take the raiders prisoner. During the night, a unit of Marines arrived under the command of Lieutenant Israel Green. In the early hours of October 18, Lee sent Stuart forward under a white flag to deliver a message to the gray-bearded leader inside the engine house. It was Brown himself who cracked open one of the oak doors and pointed a rifle at Stuart, who recognized him immediately as John Brown.

As Stuart and Brown shouted messages to each other, Stuart suddenly leaped out of the way of the door and lowered his hand that held his hat as a signal to the Marines waiting out of sight. Quickly, the military men ran forward carrying weapons and sledge hammers and began banging on one of the doors. From within the engine house, the sound of rifle fire punctuated the air along with the sounds of the heavy hammers, which had little effect on the heavy oak. Marine Lieutenant Green then ordered his men to grab a heavy, wooden ladder nearby and ram the doors. After two lunges forward, armed with the ladder, the Marines broke a large hole in one of the doors. Green, sword at his side, made his way through the opening into the smoky engine house, followed by two Marines. Both were shot immediately, one wounded in the face and the other killed. Green, meanwhile, attacked John Brown with his sword, beating him unconscious with its hilt. The fight to free the hostages was over in a matter of minutes.

The wounded Brown and his remaining followers were arrested and turned over to Virginia authorities. According to Clifford Dowdey's *Lee*, Lee's report of the incident described Brown's plan to free slaves as an "attempt of a fanatic or a madman." As for Brown, he was subsequently placed on trial for treason against the Commonwealth of Virginia. Found guilty of his crimes, Brown was hanged at the county courthouse in Charles Town on December 2, 1859.

The Approach
of War

Within a few months of the Harpers Ferry insurrection, Lee had made Arlington as close to restored as he could. Before he returned to San Antonio and to military duty in winter 1859–1860, he had Custis transferred to a posting in Washington, D.C., so that his son could keep an eye on Arlington. In San Antonio, Lee was appointed for a time as commander of the Department of Texas. There were still American Indians to pursue or negotiate with from time to time, as well as the occasional Mexican bandit. Now larger issues were at play. Returning to his former post was not the same as he had left it. The country was different after two years absent from his post.

THE THREAT OF WAR

In 1860, besides the heated arguments that raged over the power of Congress to limit slavery's expansion into the American West, or its lack of power to do so, the issue was now whether Southern states would make the fateful decision to withdraw from the Union. Throughout the year, an increasing number of Southerners had been expressing concern over the future of states rights. The year would deliver a presidential election and the Republican Party could possibly nominate a candidate who not only opposed slavery's expansion, but its continuation as an American institution. For Lee, a Southerner who supported the gradual emancipation of slaves and was against secession from the Union, the prolonged debate over slavery and its future gave him much anxiety.

Never a political individual, he watched with concern as the Democrats nominated Illinois senator Stephen A. Douglas, only to have delegates from several Southern states walk out in protest. He watched as Republicans nominated a lawyer from Springfield, Illinois, Abraham Lincoln, as their standard bearer. Southerner John Breckinridge's newly formed third party supported secession. A fourth candidate, John Bell, was a Southerner who did not want to see the South leave the fold of the United States. When Lincoln won the election that November, according to Douglas Freeman's biography, *R. E. Lee*, Lee wrote to his son:

> My only hope [is] for the preservation of the Union, and I will cling to it to the last. Feeling the aggressions of the North, resenting their denial of the equal rights of our citizens . . . I am [also] not pleased with the course of the 'Cotton States,' as they term themselves, with their selfish, dictatorial bearing. . . . While I wish to do what is right, I am unwilling to do what is wrong, either at the bidding of the South or the North.

In a series of seven debates leading up to the 1858 Illinois Senate election between Stephen A. Douglas, the Democratic incumbent, and Abraham Lincoln, the Republican candidate, the issue of slavery was of monumental importance. The legislature reelected Douglas but the debates were also a precursor to issues that Lincoln would face when the South threatened to secede from the Union.

South Carolina led the way and five other states followed, formally leaving the Union between December 1860 and January 1861. These were moves that Lee dreaded, moves that filled him with fear. In a letter featured in J. William Jones's book, *Life and Letters of Robert Edward Lee, Soldier and Man*, Lee wrote:

> I can anticipate no greater calamity for the country than a dissolution of the Union. . . . I am willing to sacrifice every-thing but honor for its preservation. . . . Secession is noth-ing but revolution. . . . A Union that can only be maintained by swords and bayonets, and in which strife and civil war are to take the place of brotherly love and kindness, has no charm for me.

Lee could take some comfort in knowing that, at least in February 1861, the legislators of his home state of Virginia voted against secession. But they also voted against going to war to restore their fellow Southern states back into the Union.

CALL TO DUTY

On March 1, 1861, Lee was asked to come to Washington to meet with General Scott about serving as Scott's aide in the war that might soon commence. A few weeks later, South Carolina forces, under the command of P.G.T. Beauregard, launched an artillery attack against Fort Sumter, one of a series of fortifi-cations built after the War of 1812. U.S. Army major Robert Anderson had secretly relocated his two companies there with-out authorization and the government of South Carolina and Rebel forces wanted them out. Lee was called again to Wash-ington to meet with Scott.

On April 18, Lee met with his old friend, Francis Blair. Blair had asked Lee to consider taking command of all fed-eral forces, effectively putting the Virginian in General Scott's place. Lee had answered clearly and firmly, as related by Lee's son, Robert Jr., in *Recollections and Letters of General Robert E. Lee*: "I declined the offer he made me to take command of the

(continues on page 54)

THE ATTACK ON FORT SUMTER

As Southern states seceded from the Union during the final weeks of 1860 and the early months of 1861, they created a problem for federal installations—forts, armories, military camps, lighthouses—that were situated on Southern soil. Would those facilities pass into the hands of the Confederacy? Was the federal government simply expected to walk away from those installations without a fight?

As Lincoln delivered his inaugural address on March 4, 1861, Confederates had already seized all but four of the following federal forts situated in the South: Fort Pickens in Pensacola Bay; two small posts in the Florida Keys; and the most significant garrison, a newly constructed fort on an island at the mouth of Charleston Harbor in South Carolina—Fort Sumter.

When South Carolina seceded on December 20, 1860, Fort Sumter still held no federal troops. On December 26, approximately 80 soldiers under the command of Major Robert Anderson, however, had taken possession of the masonry fort, under cover of darkness. On the very day of Lincoln's inauguration, he received a message from Major Anderson: If the federal government did not send supplies to Fort Sumter within weeks, the garrison would fall. Lincoln was faced with a serious decision. South Carolina sent commissioners to Washington, D.C., to negotiate the transfer of all federal property to the ownership of the newly seceded state. State officials were outraged when they learned federal forces had taken up positions within the walls of the island fortress.

Even before Lincoln took office, President James Buchanan had taken steps in support of Fort Sumter. On

(continues)

(continued)
January 5, 1861, Buchanan had dispatched an unarmed merchant ship, *Star of the West*, to Charleston, with 200 troops and supplies onboard. When word leaked out that the military vessel was headed toward Fort Sumter, South Carolinians prepared for the ship's arrival. On January 9, Charleston shore batteries opened fire on the approaching ship. When a shell scored a direct hit, the ship turned around and headed north again. Throughout the attack, Anderson held off firing the fort's guns.

Weeks passed, and the federal troops inside Fort Sumter remained hunkered down outside the harbor. On March 1, Confederate president Jefferson Davis ordered Rebel general Pierre Gustave Toutant Beauregard to take command of forces in Charleston. Four weeks later, after much debate with his cabinet members, President Lincoln ordered another ship to Fort Sumter with supplies and reinforcements. On April 12, after Lincoln telegraphed the governor of South Carolina that a resupply ship had been dispatched to Fort Sumter, Confederate batteries opened fire on the island post at 4:30 A.M. The Civil War had begun.

For nearly 34 hours, more than 3,000 Confederate shells pounded the seven-foot-thick walls of Fort Sumter. Gunners in the Union fortress managed to return fire a thousand times. When Major Anderson finally surrendered, portions of the walls had been reduced to rubble, but he had not lost a single man, only a Union horse. The first Civil War battle had been bloodless.

army that was to be brought into the field, stating as candidly and courteously as I could, that though opposed to secession
(continued from page 52)

and deprecating war, I could take no part in an invasion of the Southern States."

Immediately after meeting with Blair, Lee walked down the street a few blocks to General Scott's office. While Scott knew Blair had made the request of Lee, he did not yet know Lee's answer. When Lee informed him of his decision, Scott was disappointed, telling him: "Lee, you have made the greatest mistake of your life; but I feared it would be so." Given Lee's decision, Scott requested that his old friend resign his commission in the U.S. Army. After all, Lee would not accept a command against the South and he was a Southerner who would be privy to military information. Lee could only agree.

The U.S. government had offered Lee the command of the U.S. Army as the threat of war loomed on the horizon, and Lee had said no. It was not an easy decision to make. To remain in the uniform of the United States and lead federal forces against armies raised in rebellion by former Southern states meant that Lee, a Southerner, would be fighting his countrymen and his Southern brothers. It would mean engaging in a civil conflict that would witness American fighting American, but most importantly to Lee, he might have to fight against his fellow Virginians. In early March, Virginia had not yet seceded from the Union, and had, in fact, voted not to do so. Still, Lee understood that if war did break out between a rebel government of seceded states and the United States, Virginia might change its course in rebellion.

Prior to the Civil War, most Americans primarily identified with their region, state, or even their limited local community. Since most Americans did not regularly travel, unless they packed up and emigrated from one region to another for better opportunities, they typically formed their individual identity in more localized terms. Thus, Americans thought of themselves as northerners or southerners or easterners or westerners or by their state. For Lee to support the United States in a civil war and turn his military skills against the people of his home state was absolutely inconceivable. He resigned his commission on

In early 1861 after several Southern states seceded from the Union, General Scott offered Lee a position as top commander of the Union Army. Being loyal to his home state of Virginia, Lee turned down the offer and resigned from the U.S. Army on April 20. Soon after he took command of the Virginia state forces. Above is Lee's resignation letter.

April 20, 1861, having served in the U.S. Army for more than 30 years. As written in Charles P. Roland's *Reflections on Lee*, Lee stated: "I cannot raise my hand against my birthplace, my home, my children."

TO SERVE HIS STATE

As the war opened, the call for troops resounded across both the North and South, with Lincoln calling for 75,000 Northern volunteers and the Confederate States of America's president, Jefferson Davis, issuing the call for 100,000. Among those the South hoped would join their cause was Robert E. Lee.

On April 17, 1861, Virginia seceded from the Union. The day after his resignation, Lee attended church that Sunday morning and that afternoon a message came to Arlington asking Lee to come to Richmond to meet with Governor John Letcher. Lee agreed, knowing full well what Letcher would soon be asking of him. Virginia had joined with the states of secession, which would put Lee's home state at war. Virginia would need defending.

Letcher's offer to Lee was as straightforward as Scott's and Blair's had been: Would Lee, with the rank of major general, take command of all of Virginia's military and naval forces? This time, Lee's answer was positive. He may not have been able to take up arms within the ranks of the U.S. Army against the South and his native state, but his conscience and his loyalty to Virginia did virtually require him to say yes to defending his home state. Soon after, Lee attended the Virginia Convention, not as a soldier, but dressed in civilian clothes, where he was received with a ringing applause. Lee would lead Virginia into the war. At the convention, Lee gave the first real speech of his life, as recorded in the *Journals and Papers of the Virginia State Convention of 1861*:

> Mr. President and Gentlemen of the Convention—Profoundly impressed with the solemnity of the occasion, for which I must say I was not prepared, I accept the position assigned me by your partiality. I would have much preferred had your choice fallen on an abler man. Trusting in Almighty God, an approving conscience, and the aid of my fellow-citizens, I devote myself to the service of my native State, in whose behalf alone will I ever again draw my sword.

From that day forward, Robert Edward Lee's life would be forever redirected.

In Defense
of Virginia

In 1861, Lee was 54 years old, still distinguished and handsome, not yet sporting the full gray beard with which he is often portrayed today. He was still healthy, taller than most of his contemporaries, and solidly built. Despite his size, his feet could be considered dainty. He wore a four and a half inch shoe.

Almost immediately after accepting military duty on behalf of Virginia, Lee opened an office in Richmond, in the same building that housed the post office, and found lodging at a local hotel. The Virginia state capital was a good-sized city in 1861, with a population of nearly 40,000 people, the third largest in the South behind New Orleans, Louisiana, and Charleston, South Carolina. While Montgomery, Alabama, was originally chosen as the Confederate States' capital, once

"White House of the Confederacy," 12th and Clay Sts., Richmond, Va.

The Confederate States of America was the government set up by the 11 Southern states that had seceded from the Union from 1861 to 1865. Jefferson Davis was elected leader of the Confederacy, the Virginia State House served as the Capitol building, and the White House of the Confederacy *(above)* was located in Richmond.

Virginia seceded the capital was swiftly moved to Richmond, placing it closer to the primary action of the war as events unfolded. With its new status, Richmond was soon the center of a great bustle of political, economic, and military activity, its population swelling to more than 100,000 residents. By early 1865, 300,000 people were in Richmond, many of them refugees of the war itself.

Lee had much to do in his new role as Virginia's military leader. The state was one of the largest of all Southern states in the Confederacy, comprising a total of more than 67,000 square miles. (At that time, Virginia included what is today the state of West Virginia.) There were more than 1,100 miles of railroad to protect, plus cities and towns; harbors and shipyards; factories, foundries, and arsenals; lead mines and salt works; and farm fields, including the Shenandoah Valley, which would become the South's "bread basket."

Lee's plans included three primary objectives. First, he needed to secure Virginia's defenses; second, he needed to collect as many weapons and armaments of war as possible; and third, he needed to rally the people of Virginia with calls to duty, dedication, perseverance, and sacrifice. Otherwise, he believed, victory in this war would be impossible. Even as the war unfolded slowly during the spring months that followed the attack on Fort Sumter, Lee did not agree with sentiments on both sides that the war would be quick and decisive. He wrote to his wife, Mary, that he thought the war might drag on for at least a decade.

Lee's family, too, experienced great changes. Custis was almost 30 years old and a first lieutenant in the U.S. Army Corps of Engineers. Like his father, Custis resigned from the U.S. Army on May 2 and accepted a captain's rank in the Confederate Engineering Corps. Rooney joined the Confederate cavalry. Three of Lee's nephews joined the Confederate Navy, including West Point graduate Fitzhugh Lee. Robert Jr. continued his education at the University of Virginia. The youngest girl, Mildred, also remained in school at Winchester, Virginia, while the other girls stayed with their mother in Arlington.

Politically, remaining in her ancestral home became too difficult for Mary and the girls. In May 1861, Mary and the daughters packed up and went to live with relatives in Fauquier County, Virginia, and had to move again in the fall to Shirley Plantation, along the James River south of Richmond. During the war, Mary would be forced to move several times to remain out of harm's way and avoid capture by the enemy.

"GRANNY LEE"

May 14, 1861, Lee was appointed brigadier general by the Confederate War Department. The rank was temporary, for just two days later, the Confederate Congress advanced Lee to full general, although the change did not go into effect until August. This placed Lee third in rank among Confederate officers, behind Samuel Cooper and Albert Sidney Johnston, under whom Lee had served in the U.S. 2nd Cavalry in Texas during the 1850s. Still, much of Lee's efforts were spent behind a desk in Richmond, not in the actual field of war.

Lee did not have to wait long before President Davis relented and gave him a temporary field command. Davis dispatched Lee into western Virginia on a mission to halt the advance of Union troops that had entered the state from the west and were threatening to take control or destroy important rail lines in the region. Lee was expected to redirect Confederate forces already in the field, men serving under three different field commanders who did not get along well with one another. When Lee sent men against McClellan's forces, the Confederates were badly beaten by a Union army unit under the command of General Joseph J. Reynolds.

Lee lost the Battle of Cheat Mountain (September 10–14) for several reasons. His men were suffering at that time with a violent outbreak of the measles; poor weather conditions rendered roads muddy and almost impassable; the Confederate forces under his command were undisciplined, green troops. In addition, Lee shared command with General W. W. Loring. Loring, a younger officer, took Lee's arrival as a signal that officials in Richmond did not have faith in Loring.

It was a poor showing for Lee's first time in the field since his days in Texas. Lee was soon mocked in Southern newspapers, including the Richmond *Examiner*, which described Lee as "a general who had never fought a battle . . . and whose extreme tenderness of blood induced him to depend exclusively on the resources of strategy, to essay the achievement of victories without the cost of life." Translation: Lee was too soft on the battlefield. The papers labeled him as "Granny Lee." Although the war was only six months old, Lee's beard had already turned almost completely gray.

SERVICE IN RICHMOND

With his loss at Cheat Mountain, Lee was soon assigned to duties not directly connected to the battlefield, including work in Charleston, South Carolina, where he beefed up the port city's coastal defenses in the face of an ever-growing Union fleet. Then he was sent to Georgia and Florida to do more engineering work. During the four months that kept him busy as an engineer, he ordered so many entrenchments and defensive earthworks that critics referred to him as the "King of Spades." Much of Lee's work was important, however. His fortifications at Savannah, Georgia, helped that port remain out of Union hands until 1864.

During his tenure in Georgia, Lee visited his father's grave, the first of the children of Light Horse Harry to pay their respects at his resting place since his death 44 years earlier. Lee noted the grave's simple, even plain marble tablet and would later comment on the beauty of the wild olive hedge that surrounded the site. It was also at this same time that Lee came into possession of a four-year-old horse, for which he paid $200. The gray stallion had gone by names that included Greenbriar and even Jeff Davis. Lee renamed his new mount Traveller, and it would remain with him throughout the remainder of the war.

By early March 1862, Lee was summoned back to Richmond by President Davis. A year had passed since General Scott had asked Lee to serve as his aide in the then-approaching war. So much had happened during that year, not all favorable to the Confederate cause. Although there had been little fighting in the Eastern Theater during the winter of 1861–1862, there had been significant action out in Tennessee. A low-ranking Union general named Ulysses S. Grant, a graduate of West Point who had ranked near the bottom of his class, pulled off twin victories by capturing Forts Henry and Donelson, located just 12 miles from one another on separate rivers, the Cumberland and the Tennessee.

The taking of the forts had secured navigation on the lower portions of these rivers for federal troops and for much of western Tennessee in the following months. Southwestern Tennessee would fall under Union control after the Battle of Shiloh (April 6-7), which was another Grant victory. Shiloh also delivered another terrible loss for the Confederacy. General Albert Sidney Johnston, one of the South's best field generals and the highest ranking officer Union or Confederate, was killed on the first day of fighting, after taking a bullet behind his right knee.

THE PENINSULAR CAMPAIGN

Other factors were already plaguing the Confederate cause in Virginia. Jefferson Davis was highly criticized for his inability to stop Union forces from marching across Southern soil. Supplies were short for many field units of the Confederate Army. Many soldiers' enlistment of one-year's service was coming to an end. To top that, the Union's leading general in the east, George B. McClellan, with whom Lee had served on Scott's staff during the Mexican-American War, was ready to launch a massive campaign against Richmond. Throughout the winter of 1861–1862, McClellan had gathered a force of over 100,000 men, training, drilling, and arming them. His strategy was straightforward: He would take his men by transport vessels from Washington, D.C., down the Potomac; land them east of Richmond on a Virginia peninsula between the York and James rivers; then march them west to the Confederate capital, and with the two rivers protecting his flanks, seize Richmond, ending the war a hero. By early April 1862, McClellan began carrying out his plan, landing the first of his forces at Fort Monroe, where Lee had been posted 30 years earlier. Naturally, President Davis was concerned about McClellan's next move. He only had 60,000 men to stop him.

President Davis relied on senior officer, General Joseph Johnston (who had served with distinction in the Mexican-American and the Seminole wars), to lead the army against McClellan. Davis also turned to Lee for counsel. In a role equal to today's army's chief of staff, Lee strongly suggested that the Confederacy begin drafting soldiers. Lee knew that the North would be able to muster more men due to its larger population. Northerners numbered 22 million at the beginning of the war, while Southerners counted for approximately 9 million and nearly half of them were slaves.

STONEWALL JACKSON

Thomas "Stonewall" Jackson was one of the oddest men to serve as a high-ranking general of the Confederacy, but he was a brilliant tactician and commander. As a younger man, Jackson had attended West Point and fought in the Mexican War. Before the Civil War, he taught artillery tactics at Virginia Military Institute.

Eccentric and highly religious, his oddities included abstaining from pepper, claiming it made his left leg ache. A hypochondriac by nature, he would stand or sit bolt upright because he believed slouching cramped his internal organs. Jackson had a habit of holding up one hand to keep his body from going "out of balance." During battles, he was remembered for sucking lemons or eating peaches. A devout observer of the Sabbath, Jackson refused to send or even read a letter on Sunday. He believed his army to be an extension of God's wrath, an army of the living God.

Those who marched under Jackson did not like him. He was stern and harsh, forcing them to march daily anywhere from 25 to 40 miles. Some referred to Jackson's infantry as "foot cavalry." In Geoffrey Ward's *The Civil War: An Illustrated History*, one infantryman summed up his commander thusly: "All old Jackson gave us was a musket, a hundred rounds and a gum blanket and he druv [drove] us

While Lee's support of a draft was important, he was primarily concerned with the defense of Virginia. Richmond and Washington, D.C., are only separated by 100 miles, and he understood how vulnerable his state capital and the Confederacy's capital was. Not only was McClellan massing troops in Washington for an assault, but other Union armies

like Hell." But Jackson was brilliant on the battlefield. As McClellan moved his great force of more than 100,000 men to a Virginia peninsula in April 1862, Lee sent Jackson and 20,000 Confederates into the Shenandoah Valley to keep several other Union armies busy.

The Shenandoah Valley was rich farm country, the breadbasket of the South. The valley lay in Virginia, west of the Blue Ridge, the easternmost spine of the Appalachian Mountains. From the valley, Jackson could move about easily, using the Blue Ridge to hide his actions, then emerge into the eastern portion of Virginia to meet his enemy. Three Union armies were kept off balance by Jackson's brilliant movements.

As Jackson weaved and dodged his way up and down the Valley, Union generals were never able to predict his movements and defeat him in the field. Only once, during a March 23 engagement at Kernstown, did Jackson lose a battle during the Valley Campaign.

Jackson was philosophical as well as practical about his field tactics. Geoffrey Ward wrote that Jackson's philosophy of war was, "Always mystify, mislead, and surprise the enemy if possible; and when you strike and overcome him, never let up in the pursuit so long as your men have the strength to follow."

After Lee, Thomas "Stonewall" Jackson was the most respected commander in the Confederate Army. Serving under Lee, Jackson became known for defeating larger armies even though his forces were outnumbered and lesser supplied. After Jackson died from complications from bullet wounds, Lee was quoted as saying, "Jackson has lost his left arm, but I have lost my right."

were already in the field, one under the command of General Irvin McDowell, the federal commander at the Battle of Bull Run, the first major land battle of the war. McDowell's forces were encamped in Fredericksburg, Virginia, only 50 miles north of Richmond.

With Union armies positioned in at least two locations in Virginia, Richmond was considered extremely vulnerable in the spring of 1862. While Johnston retreated in the face of advancing Union forces along the peninsula between the James and York rivers, General Thomas "Stonewall" Jackson was on the offensive. On May 9, he fought with McDowell's army in northwestern Virginia in the Shenandoah Valley. In fact, Jackson's men spent two weeks in May fighting three different Union armies—keeping each one off balance—in an effort to keep any of them from marching south to Richmond. This extremely effective campaign by Jackson allowed Confederate forces under Johnston's command to meet McClellan's forces on the peninsula, helping to put Lee's mind a bit more at ease. This also gave Davis and Lee the opportunity to concentrate more troops against McClellan.

BATTLE OF SEVEN PINES

By the latter days of May 1862, McClellan's army had advanced, even if awkwardly, up the peninsula and were encamped within five miles of Richmond. The time had come for both sides to strike. On May 31, the battle unfolded due east of Richmond at Seven Pines, also remembered as the Battle of Fair Oaks. Overall, the battle was not well-coordinated by General Joseph Johnston. After learning that Irvin McDowell was no longer a direct threat north of Richmond, he changed his assault plan. Confederate officers sent one division off in the wrong direction, along the wrong road. A second division did not reach the battle in time to fight fully. What might have been a destructive assault by Johnston became a scattered brawl of men. The two armies battered one another, with both taking significant casualties.

Lee had left his office in Richmond on May 31 and had rode to the front with Aide-de-Camp Charles Marshall. The battle had already begun when he reached the area of engagement, and he could hear musket fire off in the distance. When Lee reached Johnston's field position, he could see that the battle was not going well. Still, Johnston did not greet Lee's arrival warmly, even though Lee only wanted to offer assistance if he was able. At one point, Johnston left his headquarters toward the front, leaving Lee behind, who could only wonder how the battle was going. Johnston had barely spoken with him.

By mid-afternoon, President Davis arrived. Soon after, Lee and Davis mounted their horses and rode toward the sounds of battle. When they reached the edge of the fight, they found chaos: lines of men were scattered about, some units were in retreat while others stayed out of the battle entirely. Evening was drawing near and the sounds of battle were beginning to subside. Suddenly, a soldier ran past Lee and Davis, informing all that General Johnston had been severely wounded and might even be dead. Lee and Davis rode forward in search of Johnston, soon spotting two staff officers carrying the wounded commander. Davis rushed forward, asking Johnston if there was anything he could do for him while Lee watched quietly as Johnston, his old comrade from earlier days, was loaded onto a wagon.

Night had fallen and all around them were the scenes and sounds of the end of a day of battle. The wounded moaned quietly, their images dimly lit by flickering lanterns. The president of the Confederacy turned to Lee, his chief of staff, and asked him to take command of the army. Lee agreed to accept command, a decision that placed him for the first time in 13 months of war, as well as 37 years as a soldier, in command of troops he would lead into battle. According to Earle Rice's *Robert E. Lee: First Soldier of the Confederacy*, when Johnston received the word of Lee's new command while lying wounded in a Richmond hospital, he told a friend: "The shot that struck me down is the best that has been fired for the Southern cause yet, for I possess in no degree the confidence of our government, and now they have in place one who does."

In Command
of History

Although General Joseph Johnston, who had known Lee since they were classmates at West Point, was certain that the appointment of his old friend was a positive move by the Confederate government, others were less certain. Union commander General McClellan noted in his personal papers that Lee was "personally brave and energetic to a fault, he yet is wanting in moral firmness when pressed by heavy responsibility and is likely to be timid and irresolute in action." Many within the Confederate officer corps would have agreed with McClellan. They had seen him in action at his desk as an engineer, not a field commander. Lee had not proven himself to them yet.

A NEW COMMAND

Lee would soon prove himself against all doubters, North and South, within weeks of the Seven Pines debacle, during a week of intense fighting on the peninsula called the Seven Days Battles (June 25–July 1, 1862). Lee, now the commander of the Army of Northern Virginia, had given constant thought to organizing a counterattack against the great Union Army McClellan had concentrated on the peninsula.

Once Lee stepped forward and took the offensive against McClellan, he did so with aggression and confidence. He sent most of his army to engage McClellan along the Union commander's right flank, which Confederate general Jeb Stuart had determined was not well protected. In fact, McClellan's forces were straddling the Chickahominy River with 75,000 to its south and 25,000 north of the river. The move was gutsy, since it meant Lee would leave a small number of men directly in McClellan's path to Richmond. If Lee had misread the Union general, all might be lost.

The Seven Days Battles began with a minor battle of Oak Grove on June 25. Each day of battle brought major engagements, as neither side broke off or retreated completely: the battle of Beaver Dam Creek in Mechanicsville on June 26, the battle of Gaines' Mill on June 27, the battle of Savage's Station on June 29, the battle of Glendale on June 30, and the final and most important fight at Malvern Hill on July 1. Throughout the week, Lee continued to push McClellan back into retreat south across the peninsula. Union forces moved back with great consistency. At Malvern Hill, Lee stumbled. The Virginia general repeatedly sent his men forward in direct frontal assaults against McClellan's well-entrenched troops, who held the high ground. Confederate infantrymen were shot to shreds. Lee had miscalculated the Union's superior artillery and expertise, and more than 5,300 Confederate soldiers (and 3,200 Union men) were killed or wounded. According to Emory Thomas' Robert E. Lee: A Biography, one of Lee's generals, D.H. Hill summed up the action that day: "It was not war. It was murder." Lee would not repeat this kind of mistake again any time soon.

The Battle of Malvern Hill, which took place on July 1, 1862, in Henrico County, Virginia, was the final battle of the Seven Days Battles. Although Lee's Army of Northern Virginia aggressively attacked the Union Army, his complex plan was poorly executed. Lee's army suffered massive casualties, thus ending the Peninsula Campaign.

The Seven Days Battles ended the Peninsula Campaign. In August 1862, by order of President Lincoln, the troops were to withdraw in order to reinforce the Army of Virginia fighting in other campaigns. Both sides suffered major casualties. Lee's army had about 20,000 casualties out of a total of about 90,000 soldiers, while McClellan's army suffered about 16,000 casualties out of a total of 105,445 men, plus the loss of 50 artillery pieces and 31,000 muskets during the months he occupied ground on the peninsula, and it all ended with a resounding strategic loss. Northern morale was crushed and, despite their victory, Confederates were stunned.

Victory had arrived, but it had exacted a terrible toll. Lee was not greatly excited about the end of the campaign. He had only managed to stop McClellan, not bring about an end to the total conflict. Within weeks of the Seven Days Battles, Lee encouraged President Davis to allow him to take the offensive with his army. Lee felt that taking the offensive against the federals was key to ultimate success in the war. If Northerners could be convinced that the South was powerful and determined enough to continue fighting and even take the war offensively northward, they might decide a protracted war could not be won.

Early fall 1862, Lee would have his first opportunity to prove his point. In the meantime, a second battle at Bull Run would soon unfold.

LEE'S LIEUTENANTS

During the early weeks following the Seven Days Battles, Lee eliminated positions within the ranks of his staff. He removed officers that he considered not as skilled as he needed and chose two generals he could trust to take command of forces that would be used on his two flanks. One, the once fun-loving 41-year-old general James Longstreet, or "Old Pete," had become a sober-minded commander, due to the deaths of three of his children within a week of each other from a scarlet fever epidemic in Richmond in January 1862. Longstreet had already proven himself extremely capable in battle. Lee increased Longstreet's command from 6 brigades to 28.

Lee's other principal general would be Stonewall Jackson. Although, Jackson had commanded poorly during the Seven Days Battles, he had done brilliantly during the Shenandoah Valley Campaign. Lee saw in Jackson a soldier who could perform brilliantly and give the enemy a difficult time on the battlefield. These two commanders—Jackson and Longstreet— would play crucial roles in battles over the following year.

SECOND MANASSAS

Before the end of August, Lee and Jackson had met up near the former Bull Run battlefield. This time the Union commander was Major General John Pope who had earlier commanded an army out west, along the Mississippi River. Pope's army consisted of three smaller armies formerly commanded by Generals Irvin McDowell, John Frémont, and Nathaniel Banks. From August 29–30, the armies engaged in a battle that would become known as Second Bull Run, or Second Manassas.

During the first day of fighting, Jackson made his army appear vulnerable, encouraging an attack from Pope. The desired Union assault followed, and Pope's men hit the Rebel line hard but failed to break it. At one point, when some Confederate soldiers ran low on ammunition, they tossed rocks at the enemy. Pope then set his sights on a second day of fighting, confident of victory. He telegraphed Lincoln, assuring him the Confederates were on the run. Pope was not aware of Lee's positions along Jackson's right flank, an intelligence mistake that would cost him.

On the morning of the August 30, Pope attacked Jackson once more. Lee sent his men forward—30,000 troops under the command of General James Longstreet—and the Rebels pushed Pope back. The scope of the battle was immense, as Longstreet's five divisions hit the Union men along a two-mile long battlefield. As the Union broke from the fight, Southern forces delivered a shower of artillery that fully insulted the retreating army. For all his confidence before the fight, Pope had completely misjudged his opposition. The failure of the Union at Second Bull Run lay at his doorstep. McClellan also could be cited for aiding in Pope's defeat. McClellan's forces had not been dispatched to the field soon enough and when they were, McClellan was uncooperative.

The battle was costly on both sides. The Union lost 16,000 men out of 65,000, while the Confederates lost 10,000 out of 55,000. While the Southern casualties were fewer than those of the North, the number was still problematic. The war could be lost in the long run simply because the Confederacy would not be able to provide enough manpower for the long haul.

Lee's Army of Northern Virginia returned as two wings to Bull Run Creek in Manassas, Virginia, to battle Union major general John Pope's Army of the Potomac in the Second Battle of Bull Run on August 29 and 30, 1862. Lee won a great victory, only suffering about 8,300 killed and wounded out of 50,000 compared to 10,000 out of 62,000 on the Union side.

Second Bull Run was, in the end, won at a high price for the Confederacy. But, looking at the tally sheet for the summer of 1862, the South had made great achievements on the battle-field, primarily due to Lee. As William Dorsey Pender notes in *The General to His Lady*, a brigadier general from North Carolina wrote home to his wife that Lee's troops had "performed the most brilliant and daring feats of generalship and soldiership ever performed. The boldness of the plan and the quickness and completeness of execution were never beaten.

Lee had immortalized himself and Jackson added new laurels to his brow."

By the final days of August, western Virginia was out from under Union control, McClellan's Peninsular Campaign had been lost, Pope was disgraced by his mismanagement of the Second Bull Run battle, Jackson had marched rings around his Union opponents, and the only Northern troops within 100 miles of Richmond, as one observer noted, were prisoners. Even the city of Washington, D.C. was in a frightfully precarious position and vulnerable to Rebel attack.

Lee was proving himself to be a bold and able commander. As for Pope, Lincoln was disappointed in him enough to reassign him to a command in Minnesota, far from the war, to deal with a recent uprising of the local Lakota Indians. Pope never fought in the Civil War again. Now with Pope out of command in the east, Lincoln had to choose another commander. After much debate within his own cabinet, Lincoln decided to tap McClellan for a second time to command the Army of the Potomac.

A NEW CAMPAIGN NORTH

Although Lee had won a great victory at Second Manassas, he wanted to follow up his two-day battle with another hard push against Pope. On August 31, several factors—a shortage of rations for his men, fatigue, and heavy rain—kept them from any immediate action. Lee also experienced a personal injury that day. Wearing a rubber poncho and rubber overalls because of the rain, Lee was talking with his staff when someone shouted that Yankee cavalry had been spotted nearby. While dismounting from Traveller, the horse reared in surprise, tearing the reins from Lee's hand. As he fumbled for them, he tripped over his rubber overalls and fell, breaking his fall with his hands. He broke a bone in one hand and sprained them both. It was a painful and probably embarrassing injury for the general, who was soon fitted for splints and a sling. For weeks afterward, Lee was unable to use his hands, even to dress him-self. He could not ride a horse, so he followed his army in a field ambulance wagon.

A CAMPAIGN TO THE NORTH

Nevertheless, Lee wasted no time formulating his next strat-egy. He would be outnumbered if he tried to attack Washing-ton, D.C., and would have to fight against a well-entrenched enemy or maybe even engage in urban fighting. Instead, he would take the war into the North, but swing wide of the U.S. capital into Maryland.

Lee knew his move into Northern territory would require more than marching. He issued Special Order No. 191, a plan which called for Major General James Longstreet to move his two divisions toward Pennsylvania, while protecting Lee's left flank. Stonewall Jackson, commanding six divisions, was to march to Harpers Ferry where a Union garrison was sta-tioned and take them prisoner. Major General Daniel H. Hill was ordered to move toward South Mountain in Virginia and cut off any Northern troop movements there. These moves would take several days, but Lee was certain McClellan would be overly cautious and take at least two weeks to catch up with him.

This time, McClellan let Lee down. The day Lee's forces entered Frederick, Maryland, McClellan ordered his army of nearly 100,000 men to pursue the advancing Rebel army. McClellan reached Frederick on the September 12, with Lee's army already gone. On the following day, a Union army unit reached a field outside Frederick where Confederates had recently camped. There a pair of Federal soldiers found three choice cigars wrapped in a piece of paper which read: "Headquarters, Army of Northern Virginia, Special Orders No. 191," signed "By command of General R.E. Lee: R.H. Chilton, Assistant Adjutant-General." The paper was turned over to the regimental commander and then made its way up the chain of command to George McClellan. The Union commander understood perfectly what the document represented. It gave him a clear picture of how completely divided Lee's army was. Historian Stephen Sears writes about McClellan's anxious response: "Here is a paper with which, if I cannot whip Bobbie Lee, I will be willing to go home." For once, McClellan had a unique advantage over Lee, but he would have to act fast.

McClellan read the discovered order on September 13, and Lee knew of its loss by the following day, having been informed through a friendly Southerner near McClellan's headquarters. With his forces already on enemy soil, Lee was having trouble. He had known, even before taking up the march into Maryland that he was short on artillery pieces and draft animals. He had picked up some additional cannon, but still lacked for horses and mules. He also lacked supplies, including food. His men were hungry and, as Emory Thomas notes in a description made by a civilian of the poor state of Lee's men:

> When I say that they were hungry, I convey no impression of the gaunt starvation that looked from their cavernous eyes. . . . I saw the troops march past us every summer for four years, and I know something of the appearance of a marching army, both Union and Southern. There are always stragglers, of course, but never before or after did I see anything comparable to the demoralized state of the Confederates at this time. Never were want and exhaustion more visibly put before my eyes, and that they could march or fight at all seemed incredible.

The description must have carried a ring of truth: Lee was facing significant desertions at that time from among his ranks and there were other problems. His generals were arguing with one another—Longstreet with John Bell Hood, Jackson with A.P. Hill—and there was even a threat of court-martial within their ranks.

On September 14, Hill was attacked at South Mountain and overwhelmed by Union forces. Alarmed, Lee immediately ordered the scattered parts of his army to return to him to Sharpsburg as quickly as possible, where he was headquartered. Lee even decided to return his army back across the Potomac to the relative safety of Virginia. Yet, when he received word that Jackson had been successful in bringing about the surrender of Union forces as Harpers Ferry and that Stonewall and his army would soon join him, Lee reconsidered, remaining on the west side of Antietam Creek, which flowed east of Sharpsburg. If there was to be a battle, Lee thought, it will be here.

Why Lee made the decision to remain in Maryland despite being outnumbered, short on supplies and rations, and in a position that placed the Potomac River at his back with only one possible ford site (Boteler's Ford) available for evacuation is unknown. Perhaps he chose to fight before he lost even more men to desertion. Since he took positions on higher ground, perhaps he thought he could pull off a victory, in reverse, of what had happened at Malvern Hill just months earlier. Maybe he thought he could win a decisive enough battle, at such a high cost of life to the Northern army, that he could see his ultimate goal—the North becoming so demoralized that its leaders would chose to end the war and let the South go its own way—to reality. He had taken his army on the offensive to the North, and he had made the decision to take a stand. Whatever else might have motivated Lee to entrench near Sharpsburg, he likely thought he had a good chance of winning the battle that would soon unfold.

ANTIETAM—THE BLOODIEST DAY

On the morning of September 17, General Joseph Hooker, sent forward on the Union's right flank, slammed into Lee's left. This would be the first of three battles on the field along Antietam Creek that day. The fighting on the Union right continued throughout the morning, with both sides gaining and losing position in a large cornfield near a simple wooden church. Lee concentrated his troops and cannon to that cornfield, hoping to crush the Federals and take the day. In doing so, he reduced his strength along other portions of his line. The cornfield battle raged through the morning, ending in a tactical stalemate.

By midday, the fighting shifted to Lee's center, along a sunken road that would be known by day's end as "Bloody Lane." Again, Lee sent most of his men and guns to this point of the battlefield. Here, Lee knew he was fighting for the life of his army. The violence was hard and bloody and concentrated in a limited area. The Confederates were almost overwhelmed along the sunken road, except that McClellan, aghast at the sheer bloodshed, pulled his forces back and did not launch a final assault that might have turned the battle into a complete Confederate rout.

The afternoon saw the fighting shift again, this time to Lee's right flank along the banks of Antietam Creek, south of Sharpsburg. Both sides struggled to gain control of a stone bridge across the creek. The North, led by General Ambrose Burnside, poured so many men toward the bridge that the Army of Northern Virginia, as earlier in the day, was nearly overwhelmed. Only when General A.P. Hill arrived with his forces, newly delivered from Harpers Ferry, was Lee able to order a counterattack that, ultimately, rescued the Confederates from annihilation.

The day had been bloody, extremely so. History counts the single day of fighting at Antietam as the bloodiest of the war. Lee had gone into the battle with 39,000 troops and ended the day with one out of every four a casualty, including 1,546 killed, 7,754 wounded, and 1,018 missing. McClellan's losses were greater, but so was the size of his army: 12,410 casualties, including 2,108 killed, 9,549 wounded, and 753 missing. These numbers were staggering at the time, to both sides. The loss of 23,000 men represented more casualties than Americans had lost during the Revolutionary War, the War of 1812, and the Mexican-American War combined. Ultimately, Lee could not continue his campaign on Northern soil. He had been beaten by McClellan, giving the North a psychological boost.

SMALLER DRAMAS AT ANTIETAM

Directing tens of thousands of men in battle requires strong nerves, a cool eye, a level head, and extraordinary attention to detail. Prior to the battle at Antietam, Lee had made a practice of giving his subordinate generals the latitude to make significant decisions and conduct movements during an engagement based on their own judgments. During Antietam, however, he directed nearly all of the troop movements himself, personally shifting his stretched forces from the cornfield to the sunken road to the bridge across Antietam Creek. Yet even during this large-scale battle, Lee was distracted several times by smaller, otherwise inconsequential, events.

At one point in the battle, during a lull in the engagement, Lee and General Longstreet were observing the distant enemy when General D.H. Hill rode up on horseback. Longstreet warned Hill to dismount, since enemy cannon fire could strike him at any moment, but Hill remained seated on his horse. Almost immediately, a Union shell struck close by, causing Hill's horse to fall forward, its front legs having buckled. His horse was unable to regain its footing, leaving Hill in an awkward position and unable to dismount, despite all effort. Although the horse was obviously injured, the sight of Hill struggling to figure out how to get off his horse, according to historian Emory Thomas, caused "a roar of laughter from the persons present," including Lee.

But one day of fighting could have easily become two. Lee believed Union forces would redouble their efforts and attack his battered troops on a second day, and he prepared for the onslaught as best he could. He could not retreat overnight

Later in the day, as Lee was on his way from one portion of the battlefield to another, he and his aides encountered a Confederate soldier carrying a pig which he had stolen from a nearby pen. The Rebel had killed the pig, having obviously left his post in the heat of battle. Lee flushed with anger. He ordered the soldier arrested and sent to Stonewall Jackson for immediate execution on grounds of desertion and stealing. Jackson chose, instead, to put the man back into the fighting at one of the hot spots along the line. The soldier proved himself during the battle and was not executed. As noted by historian James Robertson, one of Lee's staffers observed that the thief had "lost his pig but saved his bacon."

Toward the end of the afternoon at Antietam, Lee was approached by the remaining members of an artillery unit that had already lost three of its four guns, plus men and horses. The gunners wanted to know what to do next. Lee told them to return to their remaining gun and stay in the action. One of the gunners was Lee's son, Robert Jr., who according to Emory Thomas, asked his father: "General, are you going to send us in again?" His father responded with a smile, "Yes, my son, you all must do what you can to help drive these people back."

While all three incidents were minor, given the scope of the huge battle that raged that day, Lee was still a human being who could find a moment of laughter, was driven by anger, and yet remained the consummate professional even as he ordered his own son back into the heat of battle.

across the Potomac and escape—the logistics of such a retreat were simply overwhelmingly impossible. McClellan had plenty of reserve troops and could have attacked Lee's right flank on September 18, cutting Lee off from his only evacuation point—Boteler's Ford—trapping him on Northern soil and, possibly, destroying Lee's army. But McClellan was satisfied with the victory of September 17 and did not move against Lee the following day, giving Lee time to evacuate most all of his army across the Potomac over the next couple of days. Lee's campaign to the North had ended in failure. Confederates had marched into the North ten days earlier singing "Maryland, My Maryland." They now marched out with a different refrain: "Maryland, their Maryland."

Fredericksburg and Chancellorsville

W hile McClellan had failed to follow up with a second day of fighting at Antietam, he was still credited with an important victory. Lee had been driven out of Union territory and would not return for another nine months. Compounding the loss for the Confederates was a Union victory in the Western Theater at Corinth, Tennessee, on October 4, and at Perryville, Kentucky, on October 8. Lee's army had taken a beating and needed time to recover. During the days that followed the battle, Lee took the opportunity during a visit with his son Custis to dictate some letters to his daughters, Annie and Agnes. (Custis had to write them, for Lee's hands were still bandaged from his earlier fall.) President Lincoln also took the opportunity, following Antietam, to issue publicly his Emancipation Proclamation, which announced his plans to free all

Arlington House, the home of the Lees for 30 years, was occupied by Federal forces, who used it as their headquarters for officers supervising some of the forts that were part of the defenses of Washington, D.C. In 1864, General Montgomery Meigs ordered that graves of Union soldiers be placed just outside the front door of the mansion to prevent the Lees from ever returning.

slaves in Rebel territory after January 1, 1863. The war was now, in part, about ending slavery.

More hardships were to come for Lee. In October 1862, Annie, who had been living in North Carolina at the time, contracted typhoid fever. Agnes was already with her, and Mary joined her soon after receiving word. Annie died on October 20. She was 23 years old. The news was crushing to Robert E. Lee. Emory Thomas's *Robert E. Lee: A Biography* notes Lee observing a month after his daughter's death: "In the quiet hours of the night, when there is nothing to lighten the full weight of my grief, I feel as if I should be overwhelmed." There was another loss with which Lee had to cope in October 1862. He received a two-month-old letter from a relative informing him that Arlington, Mary's ancestral home, had been occupied by Federal troops.

McCLELLAN'S REPLACEMENT

While Antietam may have been a great victory to McClellan, he did not follow up on his win until weeks later. Between October 26 and November 2, he finally moved his 100,000-man army across the Potomac to give chase to Lee, who was long gone, having returned to his native Virginia. Through those intervening weeks, President Lincoln pleaded with McClellan to take his army on the offensive, but the hard-headed Union commander simply ignored Lincoln. Finally, an exasperated Lincoln relieved McClellan of his command for the second and last time. As R.U. Johnson and C.C. Buel note in *Battles and Leaders of the Civil War*, no one was more disappointed than Lee, who observed after receiving the news of McClellan's removal: "We always understood each other so well. I fear they may continue to make these changes till they find someone I don't understand." The new command went to Major General Ambrose Burnside, another West Point graduate and Mexican-American War veteran. He had also seen action at First and Second Bull Run, the Peninsula Campaign, and Antietam. In fact, Burnside had been offered command following the Peninsula failure and following Second Bull Run, but had declined both times due to his loyalty to McClellan.

As Burnside took command of the Army of the Potomac, he represented yet another hope for the North that General Lee could be defeated on his own soil. Lee's defeat was seen as crucial to the outcome of the war. Burnside's plan was simple—to advance from his camp at Warrenton, just south of Bull Run, and march to the Virginia city of Fredericksburg, halfway between the two capitals. With Fredericksburg as a base, Burnside plotted to advance on Richmond. Meanwhile, in the months following Antietam, the Army of Northern Virginia had recuperated from the engagement, tended its wounded, and recruited new manpower. By November 1862, Lee's forces numbered 72,000, divided into two corps under the commands of Longstreet and Jackson. Burnside still outnumbered Lee, however. His 106,000 soldiers represented six corps. In mid-November, Burnside's men moved to Stafford Heights on the opposite side of the Rappahannock River from Fredericksburg.

Lee had been watching Burnside's every move, as there could be no element of surprise when a battle unfolded. His troops occupied the sloping ground behind the town, along a crescent-shaped series of hills, as well as the old colonial town itself. By late November, both armies were firmly in place. Burnside prepared to cross the Rappahannock. Since no bridge existed directly in front of the town, Burnside planned to have a wooden platform built on broad-bottomed pontoon boats, a structure called a pontoon bridge. But Lee had Mississippi sharpshooters positioned in the city's buildings overlooking the river. Burnside ordered nearly 150 Union cannon aimed toward the sleepy Virginia community from across the river.

THE BATTLE OF FREDERICKSBURG

On the morning of December 11, the Battle of Fredericksburg opened with two Rebel cannon shots from Marye's Heights. Union engineers began erecting the wooden pontoon bridge, but met with heavy fire from the Mississippians in the city. Burnside ordered Union cannon to blast away at the town; still, most of the sharpshooters survived the pounding. The bridge builders were shot by the dozens while working to lay down the bridge across the 400-foot-wide river. At one point, Union general Edwin Sumner ordered his men into the pontoon boats, and they rowed to the opposite bank just below the city. Yet the Rebels extracted a heavy price for the direct Federal assault over water.

When Sumner's men reached the city, Confederate general James Longstreet ordered the sharpshooters to fall back and join their comrades commanding the heights behind the town. An unimaginative Burnside planned a direct frontal assault against several thousand Confederates defensively positioned behind a four-foot stone wall on Marye's Heights. On the morning of December 13, as a heavy fog shrouded the field, Union troops were ordered up the heights. At 10 A.M., after the fog lifted, they attacked. Geoffrey Ward's *The Civil War* describes Longstreet's observation of the advancing Union forces: "The flags of the Federals fluttered gaily, the polished arms shone brightly in the sunlight, and the beautiful uniforms of the buoyant troops gave to the scene the air of a holiday occasion rather than the spectacle of a great army about to be thrown into the tumult of battle." As thousands of Confederate muskets and cannon fired down the sloping ground, the Union men suffered thousands of casualties. Fourteen assaults were made, and each of them failed. Blue-clad bodies piled up until, as some noted, it was impossible to walk the field without stepping on corpses. As observed in Peter Earle's book, *Robert E. Lee*, the Confederate commander watched the battle from atop the hillside: "It is well that war is so terrible. We should grow too fond of it."

WINTER OF DISCONTENT

The winter of 1862–1863 would prove a difficult one for the Confederacy and for Southerners in general. The Union's naval blockade was becoming more effective and everything was in short supply. Confederate soldiers were wearing rags for uniforms and shoes were scarce. Inflation was driving the cost of goods skyward. Between 1860 and 1863, the price of flour rose by 250 percent; bacon, 800 percent; sugar, 1,500 percent and coffee was not even available. By April 1863, Richmond experienced food riots. The war had come to roost in nearly every Southern household and almost everyone had a friend, relative, or acquaintance who had been killed. Yet the war continued,

In 1863, land and slaves comprised the bulk of Southern capital. Paper currency and other forms of wealth were hard to come by. The Davis administration attempted to enact a minor tariff to pay the bills, but most states did not collect on the tax. Accumulating war debts, the Union's destruction of railroads and depots and looting of the Confederacy's land and goods, and the sinking of cotton production caused crushing inflation and the devastation of the South's economy.

although most of the fighting in the east had been postponed until spring.

Times were also difficult for the Union. Union morale had plummeted following the Virginia defeat. During the month of January 1863, Union soldiers were deserting at a rate of a hundred per day. That winter, President Lincoln relieved General Burnside of his command. Lincoln's replacement for Burnside was Joseph "Fighting Joe" Hooker. He was capable and tenacious and definitely wanted to command. Hooker spent the remainder of the winter preparing his men for the spring campaign. He made the camps more sanitary, paid the men regularly, and made food plentiful. He drilled them and instilled confidence in them. By the time he was ready for battle, Hooker's army numbered 135,000 men. Hooker's goal was clear: "My plans are perfect. May God have mercy on General Lee for I will have none."

With both armies still encamped in the vicinity of Fredericksburg, Hooker intended to overwhelm Lee with numbers. In February 1863, Lee had dispatched James Longstreet to southern Virginia with 13,000 men to secure southern rail lines and to cover supply transports. This left Lee with approximately 60,000 men—fewer than half of Hooker's number. Without more troops, Lee was in no position to launch an offensive against the Union Army. He would have to wait for Hooker to attack.

It was a short wait. Hooker planned to split his superior force into two armies, using each to move simultaneously on the Confederate rear and front. This would require three Union corps to march in a wide arc around Lee's left flank, cross the Rappahannock 20 miles upriver from Fredericksburg, cross the Rapidan River, and attack the Rebels from the rear. To cover this action, Hooker sent two Union corps across the Rappahannock south of Fredericksburg. Backup forces would remain at Falmouth, north of the town, and wait for orders. In Hooker's mind, there could be no failure. He intended to whip Lee and clear the way to Richmond.

Just weeks before the opening of the first great spring battle between Hooker and Lee, the Confederate commander fell deathly ill. Although he had never been seriously sick before, this illness came on hard. It started with a sore throat, followed by fever, overactive pulse, and pains in both his chest and arms—all indications that he was experiencing a heart attack. The illness incapacitated Lee for weeks, rendering him non-functional. Doctors poked and prodded him, until, according to historian Freeman in his book, *Robert E. Lee*, the ill general complained that his doctors "were tapping me all over like an old steam boiler before condemning it." Lee did not return to active duty until mid-April, in time for the battle that would soon begin.

CHANCELLORSVILLE

On April 27, Hooker sent 40,000 men to the northwest to swing behind Lee's left flank. The movement required three days. On April 30, Union troops crossed the Rapidan and found themselves in a thickly wooded area, dense with foliage and underbrush. Called the Wilderness, it surrounded a small community known as Chancellorsville, which consisted of little more than the Chancellor family mansion and its farm buildings. Hooker had marched with this force and was confident he had stolen a march on Lee. On April 28, Lee had been informed of Union troop movement, but he was not aware of Hooker's superior position just a few miles away.

Early on April 29, Lee was informed that Federals had crossed the Rappahannock downriver from Fredericksburg. Later that day, word arrived from General Jeb Stuart that additional forces were fording the Rappahannock upstream and crossing the Rapidan River. Lee moved his men quickly. While Lee did not know exactly what Hooker intended, by April 30 he knew the Union Army was now settled, leading Lee to surmise that the main Union assault would come from the west. He ordered the majority of his forces to move west to meet the coming Union attack.

Hooker was, indeed, moving from the west. Lee dispatched General John Bell Hood into the Wilderness to test Hooker's front lines. Several hours of fighting passed before Hooker broke off the engagement, ordering his men to pull back to their defensive positions around Chancellorsville. Hooker's move was inexplicable to his subordinate officers, some of whom questioned his decision. He assured them he had Lee just where he wanted him and was ready to face a Confederate offensive. This had not been the plan. Hooker's intentions had always been to attack Lee offensively. Just as the battle was beginning, Hooker was starting to doubt himself.

With the initiative in his hands, Lee met with his officers to plan an attack. His scouts had determined that Hooker's line was weakest at his right flank, since its back was to the Confederates. Stonewall Jackson stepped forward and proposed a 14-mile march through the Wilderness undergrowth along a narrow trail unknown to Union troops. The move would further split Lee's forces, which were already badly outnumbered. If Jackson took 25,000 into the woods away from Lee's remaining 20,000 and the Federals discovered it, 70,000 Northern troops would easily crush the Rebels. Still Lee was up to the gamble.

At dawn on the morning of May 2, Jackson's men began their secret march. It was nearly impossible for thousands of Confederates to move through the thick underbrush of vines, thickets, and thorns without making noise. Throughout the day, Union scouts reported a Confederate presence in the woods. Although Hooker did send word to his right flank commander, Major General Oliver Howard, to tighten up his position and expect trouble, Howard did little more than reposition two infantry regiments and some artillery. In time, Hooker decided the movement indicated the Confederates were in full retreat. He was, however, greatly mistaken. By 5 P.M., just as many of the Union men were sitting down for coffee and supper, Jackson's men came bounding out of the Wilderness, their clothes torn to shreds from thorns and brambles. Catching the Northern troops completely off guard, Hooker's right flank crumpled within 15 minutes.

Although an all-out attack on Lee probably would have been successful, Hooker continued to pull his men back. Even with the arrival of an additional 20,000 fresh Union troops, Hooker never moved to the offensive. Meanwhile, on the evening of May 2, Stonewall Jackson was accidentally shot by bullets fired by Confederate pickets. He would never recover from his wounds.

The Chancellorsville battle continued without Jackson. On the morning of May 3, General Stuart took up the Confederate assault. The attack was as successful as Rebel efforts had been the previous day. During the morning battle, General Hooker, while standing on the porch of the Chancellor mansion, was wounded when a Confederate shell shattered a pillar next to him, knocking him nearly unconscious. Groggy and unfocused,

"LET US CROSS OVER THE RIVER"

Lee had gained a great victory in the battle of Chancellorsville, but the field of battle had been won at great cost, with 12,700 men counted as casualties. The most crucial among them was the loss of Stonewall Jackson.

Jackson had been wounded on the evening of May 2, following his successful advance through the Wilderness and the early evening attack on Hooker's right flank. In the darkness, around 9 P.M., Hooker and a group of staff officers and couriers had ridden along the Orange Plank Road just a mile from Hooker's headquarters at Chancellorsville. When cannon fire struck the road, Jackson and his men rode into the thick forest. This move placed the Confederate officers near Rebel picket lines. Out of the darkness, picket fire struck the horsebound Confederate officers. One of Jackson's men shouted to the confused pickets, "Cease firing! You are firing into your own men!" Disbelieving the order, the pickets fired again, this time hitting Jackson three times—once in the right hand and twice in the left arm. Jackson's frightened horse

Hooker let hours pass before he gave up command. When he did, he advised his replacement to continue the Union retreat. Less than an hour later, at 10 A.M., Lee's entire army was united and prepared to launch a full-fledged attack against a superior number of Union troops. He then received intelligence that Hooker's men had advanced on Fredericksburg and were on their way to Chancellorsville *en masse*. The wily Rebel commander met them in the field near Salem Church, Virginia, and succeeded in pushing them back. This engagement would be the last of Lee's great tactical victories.

turned toward Union lines, galloping toward the enemy. Several low tree branches nearly knocked the wounded general off his horse before a staff member stopped the blind gallop.

The wounds were severe. Hours later, field surgeons removed Jackson's arm. Two days later, the general was removed from the field and sent to recover at Guiney's Station, Virginia. He seemed to be recovering well through the following days, until May 7 when he was diagnosed with pneumonia. Three days later, the fiercely religious Confederate general died. His final words were as poignant as they were curious, words recalled in Peter Earle's biography *Robert E. Lee*: "Let us cross over the river and rest under the shade of the trees."

Lee was devastated, as was the entire Confederacy. Historian Robert Dabney notes Lee's famous words in *Life and Campaigns of Lieut.-Gen. Thomas J. Jackson*: "[Jackson] has lost his left arm, but I have lost my right." Just two months later, on the battlefield of Gettysburg, Lee would fully understand the truth of his words.

While limited fighting continued on May 4, the battle was effectively over. Outnumbered throughout the struggle, Lee had met Hooker's superior force with brilliance, daring, and tenacity. The three-day engagement resulted in nearly 30,000 casualties—12,700 Confederate and 17,200 Union. Despite Lee's tactical victory, his losses on the field were more than his army could bear. As for Hooker's men, they had listened to their commander's assurances that victory would be theirs come spring. In the heat of battle, Hooker had wilted, his courage leaving him in the early stages of command, a command that had placed him toe-to-toe with the South's best—Robert E. Lee.

"The Enemy Is There"

In the follow-up to Lee's superb victory against Union forces led by General Hooker, the military mastermind approached President Jefferson Davis with a plan that had been attempted earlier in the war. Just as Lee had proposed marching into Maryland after Second Bull Run, he now met with Davis and his cabinet to discuss a Northern campaign.

TO THE NORTH AGAIN

Selling his plan again was not easily done. Lee did have compelling reasons for wanting to launch such a daring mission. Despite battlefield victories, the South faced the problem of limited manpower. In time, there would not be enough fresh Rebel troops or the supplies to keep them in the field, while the North could hold out for much longer. Lee's army was facing supply shortages, and a Northern attack could yield new sources for the things Lee needed to keep his army going. If his men marched into Pennsylvania, they could raid the farms and small towns, and resources would be plentiful.

Some of President Davis's cabinet members opposed Lee's proposal, claiming, and rightly so, that Richmond would be vulnerable to attack. The suggestion was made to have some of Lee's troops transferred to the Western Theater where General Ulysses S. Grant was laying siege to Vicksburg, one of the few remaining Confederate positions on the Mississippi River. Still Lee's plan was approved, but first Lee had the sad duty of replacing Stonewall Jackson. Ultimately, Jackson's men were divided into three corps under the commands of Generals Longstreet, A.P. Hill, and Richard S. Ewell. Then Lee ordered his men to march north on June 3, 1863.

Major General Hooker, having received information that Lee was on the move, requested orders to follow the Confederate army. But Lincoln had lost confidence in Hooker and refused his request. On June 9, however, Hooker gained access to information picked up by the Federal cavalry. Where Union cavalry had crossed the Rappahannock River in order to see where Lee was moving, mounted units had caught Jeb Stuart's cavalry off guard and engaged them in battle at Brandy Station, Virginia. This led to the largest cavalry battle of the entire war, involving thousands on both sides in close hand-to-hand combat with handguns and sabers. Stuart alone had gathered 9,000 cavalrymen at Brandy Station before the battle broke out.

When the engagement opened, Lee rode to the battle scene and even watched some of the battle from the rooftop cupola of a house close to the battleground. Later in the day, he went down closer to the scene and found his son Rooney wounded from a bullet to the leg. Lee was relieved the wound was not any more serious than it was. While the battle was a technical draw, with both sides bloodying one another, it also gave Lee's

Union general George Meade replaced Major General Joseph Hooker as commander of the Army of the Potomac after Hooker proved to be too timid. July 1–3, 1863, Meade's army battled Lee's Army of Northern Virginia in the Battle of Gettysburg, where he won the battle that is considered the turning point of the war.

general location and intent away. Following the battle, Hooker was informed that Lee was moving north.

Hooker's initial response was to wire Lincoln and suggest that he lead his army to Richmond once and for all. Since this would leave Washington, D.C., vulnerable, Lincoln vetoed the plan, telling Hooker, as noted in Roy Basler's *The Collected Works of Abraham Lincoln*: "I think Lee's army, and not Richmond, is your true objective point." With 85,000 men under his command, Hooker pursued the Rebel army.

Lee's forces crossed the Potomac River and reached Pennsylvania by mid-June. By June 27, Lee's main column of 65,000 men had reached the small town of Chambersburg. They raided the town's stores and stole shoes, clothing, and food. In the neighboring town of York, Lee's men took $28,000 from the local bank. Meanwhile, Hooker's men began crossing the Potomac. Nevertheless, officials in the War Department, uncertain of Hooker's ability to command given the Chancellorsville loss, requested that he resign his command. His replacement was a reluctant but willing Major General George G. Meade, the commander of the 5th Regiment, who was unprepared for what lay ahead. Hooker had developed no strategy and was uncertain of Lee's location.

THE BATTLE UNFOLDS

In late June, both Rebel and Union forces were uncertain of each other's locations. On June 23, Lee dispatched General Stuart to gather intelligence concerning the approaching Union army, but when he did not hear from Stuart for several days, Lee believed the Federals were still a great distance away. On June 28, a civilian spy reported to Lee that Union forces were north of the Potomac, near Frederick, Maryland. Alarmed, Lee hastily sent forces to Cashtown, nine miles west of a sleepy little junction called Gettysburg. Lee knew he was in no position to fight a battle at that point, for his 75,000 men were scattered out along a road over a distance of 100 miles.

Lee heard of Meade's taking command on June 29, which concerned the Confederate commander. That day, as noted in Emory Thomas's *Robert E. Lee: A Biography*, he told his lieutenants: "Tomorrow, gentlemen, we will not move to Harrisburg, as we expected, but will go over to Gettysburg and see what General Meade is after." Lee also remarked: "General Meade will commit no blunder in my front, and if I make one he will make haste to take advantage of it." By the following day, Meade's advance forces had reached the outskirts of Gettysburg, as Meade had dispatched Brigadier General John Buford's cavalry into Gettysburg in search of rebel forces.

Gettysburg had not been part of either army's plans as they advanced across southern Pennsylvania. Yet with at least 10 roads in the region converging at or near this small Pennsylvania town, it was inevitable that both armies would end up there. Early on the morning of July 1, Confederate troops advanced into Gettysburg in search of enemy troops and a cache of shoes rumored to be stored there. From a high point near the city, Rebels spotted the advance of Buford's cavalry. Messengers sent word to General A.P. Hill, who took the information to Lee. The greatest fight of the war was about to begin. It would stretch over the first three days of July as two massive armies hurled themselves at each other with deadly fury. General Lee fought the battle with three large troop units, under the commands of Longstreet (Corps I); Richard S. Ewell, whom many referred to as "Old Baldhead" (Corps II); and Ambrose P. Hill (Corps III). Meade commanded a total of seven corps at Gettysburg.

The two armies clashed at 4 P.M., just as Hill's units attacked the Federal 1st Corps. Between Ewell's forces and Hill's forces, the Union armies were pushed south of the town where they took up positions on the rise of Cemetery Hill. Although some of Ewell's subordinates wanted to continue the attack despite the late hour, Ewell chose to halt the battle, claiming he did not have orders from Lee. Lee, in fact, had instructed Ewell to take

Cemetery Hill "if possible." Ewell's reluctance may have cost them Confederate victory at Gettysburg.

GETTYSBURG, DAY TWO

Throughout the night of July 1-2, both armies feverishly moved their forces into position, working under the light of a full moon. Lee had won, overall, the first day's fight, which included taking 5,000 Union soldiers prisoner. Still, the high ground and who held it was really what mattered during the next two days of fighting. General Meade, holding the ridges and hills south of Gettysburg, positioned his men along Culp's Hill, Cemetery Hill, and south along Cemetery Ridge. With Union units in place, Lee had little choice but to configure his men similarly facing the well-entrenched federals. On the morning of July 2, Lee was determined to hit the Union line hard. His men were dispatched to attack both the Union left and right flanks. Lee ordered General Longstreet to move forward through the night to Seminary Ridge, a hill which parallels Cemetery Ridge to the west.

Longstreet, from the moment he arrived at the Gettysburg field, was opposed to the Army of Northern Virginia fighting a battle there. The Federals held the high ground from the beginning, making the field a terrible one for the Confederates. He studied the lay of the land and the army's options and told Lee of his alternative plan, according to Bevin Alexander's *Robert E. Lee's Civil War*:

> All we have to do is to throw our army around by their left [south], and we shall interpose between the Federal army and Washington. We can get a strong position and wait, and if they fail to attack us we shall have everything in condition to move back tomorrow night in the direction of Washington.

But Lee would not hear the strategic logic in Longstreet's plan. "No," said Lee, "the enemy is there, and I am going to attack him there. . . . They are there in position, and I am going to whip them or they are going to whip me."

Longstreet gave Lee his observed answer: "If he is there tomorrow, it will be because he *wants* you to attack him."

Lee would get his way. Historians continue to contemplate why Lee chose to remain at Gettysburg to fight, given that the Federals had the superior ground.

Even as Longstreet organized his men on July 2 for their assault on the Union's flanks, Jeb Stuart finally reported in, too late to make any real difference. Lee was not pleased, having already fought for two days without knowing the strength or position of Union troops. As Emory Thomas notes, Lee's response to Stuart's tardy return was straightforward and cold: "Well, General Stuart, you are here at last."

Yet Stuart was hardly to blame for Lee's predicament. Lee's decision to fight at Gettysburg against the fervent reservations of General Longstreet was one of the poorest of his command.

While Lee gave orders for Longstreet to lead the attack, by dawn on July 2, only two of Longstreet's three divisions had even reached Seminary Ridge. Then, a series of delays postponed the assault until 4 P.M. Historians have accused Longstreet of moving too slowly on the second day of fighting at Gettysburg, given his opposition to engaging the Union Army at Gettysburg on a field of their choosing. He tried to encourage Lee to abandon the field, arguing Union forces would give chase, leaving Lee free to select the battlefield of his choice. But Lee, both physically ill and tired of war, was determined to fight Meade at Gettysburg. The decision would become one of the most controversial of Lee's career.

When Longstreet's men finally attacked the Union left flank, they met the Federal 3rd Corps under the command of Major General Daniel Sickles, who had been ordered to hold his position along the left flank at the base of Cemetery Ridge. But Sickles chose to move his men forward, leaving a hole in Meade's defensive line. By the time Meade realized Sickles' unauthorized move, it was too late. For three hours, some of the most intense fighting of the war took place along the Union left flank. But the key to holding the Union line fell to the 20th Maine Infantry Regiment, which was sent up a short hill at the end of the Union left flank, under the command of Colonel Joshua Lawrence Chamberlain to hold the hill. While Sickles had mismanaged his place on the battlefield, Chamberlain and the few hundred men under his command, held their positions tenaciously. Along with strong resistance on the Union's right flank that day, Meade was able to stand against the fury of Lee's forces. As for Sickles, his corps was so badly destroyed that day it was soon disbanded and their commander suffered a severe wound resulting in the removal of his right leg.

PICKETT'S CHARGE

Longstreet's troops fought hard on July 2, yet the outcome of the battle was still to be decided. Early on the morning of July 3, Lee proposed his plan of attack. Confederate cannon were to be concentrated on the center of the Union line, where Lee suspected the enemy would be weak. Following a lengthy cannon barrage, one of Longstreet's divisions, under the command of Major General George E. Pickett, was to march nearly a mile across an open field straight into the heart of the Union line. To Longstreet, the plan was madness. After Lee completed his presentation, Longstreet expressed his doubts, according to Emory Thomas's *Robert E. Lee*:

> That will give me fifteen thousand men. I have been a soldier, I may say, from the ranks up to the position I now hold. I have been in pretty much all kinds of skirmishes, from those of two or three soldiers up to those of an army corps, and I think I can safely say there never was a body of fifteen thousand men who could make that attack successfully.

Impatient, Lee informed Longstreet he wanted his orders obeyed.

After Confederate attacks had failed the day and night before on the Gettysburg battlefield, Lee ordered an assault against the Union center position on Cemetery Ridge on July 3, 1863. Major General George Pickett led the charge, which is now called Pickett's Charge. The attack was considered a major mistake by Lee, with over 50 percent casualties on the Confederate side.

After noon on July 3, hundreds of Confederate cannon opened up a massive artillery barrage on the Union center line, firing from positions along Seminary Ridge. From 1 P.M. until around 2:30 P.M., the roar of the massed cannon split the open sky above Gettysburg. The air grew so thick with smoke, Confederate gunners could not see if they were hitting their intended marks. While early Rebel cannon shots did some damage, repeated firings dug the guns' wheels into the ground, causing the shots to arc behind the Union troops massed behind a long, stone wall.

By 2:30, the cannon barrage halted, and an eerie silence fell across the battlefield. General Lee ordered Longstreet to assemble Pickett's division of 13,500 men for an open ground march toward the Union center. An eager Pickett was delighted to lead the charge. As Confederate troops marched across nearly a mile of exposed field, Union guns opened fire, cutting them down

VICTORY AT VICKSBURG

Lee's desperate battle plan had failed with the defeat of Pickett's Charge. More battles took place on July 3, including a massive cavalry engagement between Jeb Stuart's horsemen—who had only reached Gettysburg at the end of the previous day—and Michigan troops under the command of a young general named George Armstrong Custer. But Stuart was no more successful than Pickett. There was nothing left to do but to try to escape to avoid the total annihilation of his army.

But no Union counterattack took place. Meade, a naturally cautious commander who had only replaced Hooker days before the Gettysburg battle, refused to advance against a weakened Lee, despite the fact that he still had tens of thousands of fresh reserve troops. It was a decision that Lincoln would regret. Historian James McPherson reveals Lincoln's frustration: "We had them in our grasp," Lincoln lamented. "We had only to stretch forth our hands and they were ours. And nothing I could say or do could make the Army move."

Gettysburg was one of the costliest battles of the Civil War. These were losses from which Lee could not easily recover. Yet Confederate resolve was strong. As one of Lee's men put it, as noted by historian Geoffrey Ward: "We'll fight them, sir, till hell freezes over, and then we'll fight them on ice!"

The Union's Gettysburg victory was celebrated across the North. This important win was soon joined by another

by the dozen. At first, Pickett's men moved in a steady march, then a trot, then all began to run toward the waiting enemy, shouting the Rebel yell and waving their battle flags.

Northern victory along the banks of the Mississippi River out in the war's Western Theater. On May 14, nearly two months earlier, General Ulysses S. Grant had captured Jackson, Mississippi, opening the way for the capture of one of the final Confederate blocks to Union traffic on the Mississippi River—Vicksburg, Mississippi. On May 16, as Grant's forces marched toward Vicksburg, a Confederate army of 20,000 under the command of John C. Pemberton engaged Grant at Champion's Hill, just west of the coveted city. Failing to halt Grant's advance, Pemberton struck again the next day and this time was forced to retreat with his troops to Vicksburg.

For the next six weeks, Grant laid siege to the city. Inside, the city's civilian population experienced the horrors of mortar bombardments and a dwindling food supply. They dug caves and tunnels into hillsides to serve as bomb shelters. In the final days of the siege, soldiers and civilians alike were forced to eat mule meat, household pets, even rats. The only Rebel army close enough to relieve those trapped at Vicksburg was simply too small to face Grant's combined force of 70,000 men.

On July 3, the final day of the Battle of Gettysburg, many of Pemberton's besieged soldiers sent him a petition stating, as noted by historian Allan Nevins: "If you can't feed us, you had better surrender." On July 4, Pemberton did just that. As word spread down river, another Confederate holdout, Port Hudson, surrendered to Union forces on July 8. For the first time during the Civil War, the Mississippi River was solidly in Union hands.

The Union troops were gathered behind the wall anxiously watched the advancing Confederates. As the enemy drew closer, one unit of Union troops, the 71st Pennsylvania, situated along a 90-degree turn in the wall called "The Angle," cut and ran in the face of thousands of wildly screaming Rebels. Some of the Southern troops reached The Angle, but they were driven back almost immediately. Those who reached the wall were either killed or captured. Pickett's Charge ended in bloody disaster.

When the retreat was completed, only 7,000 of those who had marched against the Union line returned. As Lee watched, the stragglers wearily retreated past him. On horseback the Confederate commander rode up and down the line, talking to the soldiers he had just sent up Cemetery Ridge into the face of enemy guns. Emory Thomas notes Lee's desperate words:

> All this will come right in the end; we'll talk it over afterwards; but, in the meantime, all good men must rally. . . . General Pickett, place your division in the rear of this hill, and be ready to repel the advance of the enemy. . . . Your men have done all that men could do; the fault is entirely my own. . . . Never mind, General, all this has been my fault—it is I that have lost this fight and you must help me out of it the best way you can.

The fate of the Battle of Gettysburg had been determined. Over 5,600 of Lee's soldiers were killed or wounded during the afternoon charge. Out of 38 Confederate battle flags going into Pickett's Charge, the Union had captured 30. Pickett's Charge had not taken more than an hour, but it was over, and Lee needed to shift to a new strategy of retreat. There was nothing left for him to accomplish on Cemetery Ridge. The only question was whether General Meade would let him retreat. Between the two armies, 50,000 soldiers had fallen during the three days of battle. Meade would not be inclined to stretch the battle into a fourth day.

That evening went long, with Lee meeting at Hill's head-quarters, then back to his own, arriving toward 1 A.M. Historian Thomas relates how Lee appeared to a cavalry officer who was present at Lee's arrival:

> He was almost too tired to dismount. The effort betrayed so much physical exhaustion that I hurriedly rose and stepped forward to assist him, but before I reached his side he had succeeded in alighting, and threw his arm across the saddle to rest, and fixing his eyes upon the ground leaned in silence and almost motionless upon his equally weary horse,—the two forming a striking . . . group. The moon shone full upon his massive features and revealed an expression of sadness that I had never before seen upon his face.

Lee remained fixed in that position for a minute or two, then turned to the officer and spoke:

> I never saw troops behave more magnificently than Pickett's division of Virginians did to-day in that grand charge upon the enemy. And if they had been supported as they were to have been—but, for some reason not yet fully explained to me, were not—we would have held the position and the day would have been ours . . . Too bad! Too bad! OH! TOO BAD!

After those words, Lee composed himself and invited the cavalry officer into his tent to look at some maps. The retreat would begin soon. Two days following the fateful tragedy of Pickett's Charge, Lees army began their sorrowful march back to Virginia in a hard downpour.

Lee and Grant

W hile the spring of 1863 had delivered Rebel victories, overall the war was going badly for the South. There were manpower shortages, munitions were running low, and the Union blockade of Southern ports was largely complete. With major Union victories at Vicksburg, Port Hudson, and Grant's brilliant generalship along the Tennessee River, the South's chances of winning the war were dwindling. As July 4, 1863, dawned, Lee had been defeated at Gettysburg. The Virginia general was downhearted and even questioned whether he should continue to lead the Army of Northern Virginia. When he offered to resign, President Davis would not consider it. Davis even suggested that if Lee was replaced, the whole Southern army would rebel against him.

A WINTER OF LOSS

Lee spent the remainder of the summer after the Gettysburg loss trying to recover. Although the Virginia army was not fighting any longer, battles were taking place elsewhere, and the South was not doing well. At one point, President Davis even suggested to Lee that he take part of his army out to the Western Theater to bolster the Confederate Army of Tennessee, but Lee would not leave his home state, although he did send some of his men west with General Longstreet.

In September, a large fight in northern Georgia pitted Northern and Southern forces against one another. The Battle of Chickamauga, fought September 19–20 and included Longstreet's men, ended with a Southern victory of sorts for the Confederates, while resulting in thousands of casualties. But the follow-up engagement, the Battle of Chattanooga two months later, delivered a crushing defeat for the Confederates at the hands of the Union Army under the command of General Grant. The Union victory not only meant Northern control of eastern Tennessee, it also produced nearly 7,000 Confederate casualties. The battle also caused President Lincoln to promote General Grant to commander of all the armies of the United States. By February 1864, the U.S. Congress resurrected the former grade of lieutenant general, and Grant received his commission on March 9.

The winter of 1863–1864 proved extremely difficult for the Confederacy in general and upon Lee specifically. He saw the signs everywhere that the Southern cause was failing. The entire Mississippi River Valley was in Federal hands, as well as all of Tennessee. The southern coast was being strangled by the ever-expanding Union naval blockade. Much of the Northern reaches of Lee's Virginia were scorched from war, and fields were barren. Ill-fed, ill-clothed Confederates tried to survive without freezing or starving. James Robertson writes

Religion played a great role in the Confederate Army due to the profound stresses on the Southern soldier. Several large religious revivals swept through the Army of Northern Virginia in the winter and spring of 1863, and historians estimate that about 150,000 soldiers were converted that year. Pictured is a group that includes wounded soldiers in front of the United States Christian Commission office.

in *Virginian Soldier, American Citizen: Robert E. Lee* that Lee, told the Confederate secretary of war that in January: "Unless there is a change, I fear the army cannot be kept effective and probably cannot be kept together." The desperation of the Confederate Army led to many religious revivals, as soldiers turned to God in search of comfort and reassurance. Historians estimate that 15,000 Confederates converted to some form of the Christian faith that winter.

Winter gave Lee the opportunity to visit with his family periodically. Still, when he did gather with his wife and children, it was difficult for them to be truly joyous. Their home, Arlington, had been confiscated by the Federals and turned into a cemetery. Mary was riddled with arthritis. Daughter Annie was dead. Agnes's suitor had been killed in recent fighting. And Lee himself, the formerly dashing, handsome Virginian, was aging fast, his hair and full beard a snowy white. He struggled with rheumatism and a pain that constantly racked the left side of his body.

Through that long, cold winter, though, the vast majority of Lee's men stuck by him, remaining in their makeshift encampments as they fought the hardships along with their general. Lee remained in constant contact with his soldiers, riding Traveller often through their ranks and into their camps. He wanted them to know that he cared and that he was doing as well for them as he could. Finally spring arrived, and Lee soon faced a new challenge—General Ulysses S. Grant.

THE CLASH OF TITANS

Once Grant gained command and was transferred to the Virginia theater, he proposed a broadbased offensive, using the North's superior numbers to attack the Confederacy on multiple fronts and bring the South to its knees. His plan had three parts: the Federal Army of the James (River), consisting of 30,000 men, was to advance up the James River toward Richmond. From Chattanooga, Tennessee, Union general William Tecumseh Sherman was ordered to march south toward Atlanta to destroy the strategic Southern center. As for Grant, he would march with Meade's army, and their target would be Lee's Army of Northern Virginia. For virtually the first time during the war, Union armies would move in sync, their efforts coordinated and overlapping.

There were also lesser goals and campaigns: A Union army was dispatched into the Shenandoah Valley to destroy the South's "bread basket". Another Union force was sent to attack Mobile, Alabama, the only remaining southern port in the Gulf region still not under federal control. An additional Northern unit was ordered to secure the part of Louisiana not under the

Union's authority. Everywhere across the South, Grant was delivering the terrible and swift sword of Northern military power against the weakened Confederacy.

By May 1864, Grant prepared to meet Lee in the field for the first time. The stakes were high. Grant understood that not only must Lee be defeated (other Union generals, including McClellan and Meade had managed that), but his army had to be completely destroyed. That month, the Union Army of 120,000 and Lee's of 65,000 were encamped near the Rappahannock, outside Fredericksburg, in the vicinity of Chancellorsville—a field littered with the skulls of previously fallen soldiers.

Lee did not take Grant for granted. He had watched throughout the previous years of war as Grant made a name for himself by winning repeated victories at Forts Donelson and Henry, at Shiloh and Vicksburg, and Jackson and Chattanooga. Grant had become legendary, perhaps unstoppable.

On May 4, Grant sent Meade's forces into the same heavy woods that had been the site of the Chancellorsville battle a year earlier. Grant planned to move his left flank in the vicinity of the Confederate right, always in the direction of Richmond, as he was certain that Lee would keep his army between Union forces and the Rebel capital. By this tactic, Grant could antici-pate where battles would take place, while moving ever closer to Richmond. Fighting in the Wilderness began on the morning of May 5. Here, Lee could fight without worrying about Grant's superior numbers, since mobility and military lines would be nearly impossible. Fighting among the tangled underbrush and hanging grapevines of the Chancellorsville woods was nightmarish. Troops got lost amid the heavily wooded growth, smoke, and fires from exploding shells and muzzle flashes. Wounded soldiers, unable to move, were burned alive by the dozens. After a day of back-and-forth fighting, both armies broke off, with no clear winner.

The following day, fighting resumed, with Union troops advancing. As the outcome of the battle tipped, Lee feared defeat. Bravely, the valiant Confederate general came forward and tried to lead troops from the front, putting himself directly in harm's way. But his men would have none of it. As recounted by Gene Smith in *Lee and Grant*, Confederates virtually encircled their commander, shouting: "Go back, General Lee. Lee to the rear." A Rebel sergeant grabbed Traveller's reins to stop his general's advance. "Go back, General Lee, this is no place for you; we'll settle this." As Lee shouted, "Charge! Charge, boys!", his men continued their shouts: "Go back, General Lee! Go back! We won't go on unless you go back!" Lee finally withdrew from the heat of the battle.

On the brink of victory, Union forces again lost their way in the forest. Confederates, meanwhile, having been reinforced by Longstreet's men, pushed forward, throwing back the Union right flank. During the battle, Longstreet was wounded by friendly fire. After two days of fighting, the Confederates had managed to turn the Federal flanks and had inflicted 17,000 casualties against the enemy, compared to 11,000 for Lee's forces. Many longtime Union veterans believed the battle was over, that they had lost again, and tomorrow would involve a retreat north. But Lee's victory was not that simple nor that decisive, not to Ulysses Grant. Both sides were surprised when, on the morning of May 7, Grant prepared to engage the enemy yet again, moving his men south, by his left flank, toward Richmond. The new leader of the Army of the Potomac had no intention of quitting the fight.

Grant's next plan was to engage Lee at the only spot possible, given the roads and the lay of the land—Spotsylvania Courthouse—just a few miles from the Wilderness. Lee knew this would be the next site of battle and ordered his men to build entrenchments and breastworks for protection against the coming assault. By the morning of May 8, those entrenchments stretched on for five miles.

SPOTSYLVANIA AND COLD HARBOR

The battle for Spotsylvania opened on May 9 with Grant's forces pounding Confederates for nearly two weeks. On the fourth day, Union assaults broke the enemy's resistance, and Federal troops rounded up 4,000 Rebel prisoners and 20 Southern cannon. The breach in the Confederate line again caused Lee to try to field command directly, but his men rallied and pushed Union forces back. The fighting was desperate. Confederate entrenchments formed a V shape. It was there that Union forces broke the Rebel line. At this "bloody angle," the fighting approached complete frenzy. At some spots, the dead and wounded piled up three deep. Although heavily pressed, Lee's lines held.

The fighting of May 10–12 was the most intense of any at Spotsylvania. Union casualties amounted to 18,000 men, while Lee lost 12,000. One of the most significant losses Lee suffered was the death of his great cavalry commander, General Jeb Stuart. Grant had earlier ordered his chief cavalry officer, Phil Sheridan, to swing his mounted troops wide around Lee's flank. Stuart's men had met Sheridan's challenge and chose to block the Union cavalry in an engagement at Yellow Tavern just six miles outside of Richmond. During the fighting on May 11, Stuart was struck down by an enemy bullet. He was carried from the field of battle by his comrades, whom he asked to sing "Rock of Ages" to comfort him. The 31-year-old Irish cavalry commander died the following day. When Lee received the news of the death of his scout, he was nearly without words. Recalled by historian Gene Smith, Lee stated: "I can scarcely think of him without weeping."

After a week of heavy fighting, Lee was faced with the prospect of his defeat. In a war based on sheer numbers, he knew he could not win. After May 12, the fighting continued, but at a lesser intensity. After another week, Grant ordered his army to move again by the left flank, closer to Richmond. Lee moved accordingly to a locale 20 miles to the south, where he entrenched his men behind the North Anna River. Here, Grant chose not to fight, for the field had been of Lee's choosing. Instead, he flanked the Confederates again, and crossed

Generals Grant and Lee met again at the Battle of Spotsylvania Court House (May 8-21), a few days after the bloody Battle of the Wilderness. The Union Army numbered about 111,000 men while the Confederate Army had little over 63,000. By the end of this battle, the Confederate Army took on more heavy losses and the Union Army was closer to the Confederate capital of Richmond.

the Pamunkey River on May 28. Here, he met the Rebels entrenched behind Totopotomy Creek. Richmond was just 10 miles to the southwest. Again, Grant slipped to the left. Again, Lee moved ahead of is enemy, taking up positions at a cross-roads called Cold Harbor.

When the morning of June 2 broke, it was hot and humid. Grant ordered a full attack on Lee's positions, hoping to strike before the Confederates had completed their entrenchments. But many of his men had not even arrived at Cold Harbor and one corps got lost. Nearly all of his men were bone-weary, unable to remain awake. The attack was postponed by another day. Unfortunately, this provided time for Lee's men to fortify a six-mile long entrenchment, with rivers protecting both flanks.

As his men prepared their entrenchments, Lee rode up and down his lines on Traveller, wearing a nonmilitary issue sack linen coat because of the humidity. He expected an attack at any time, even though he was still waiting for several brigades to reach the line and take their places. They finally showed up around 10 A.M. Morning slipped into afternoon, and a gentle rain cooled the field and the men who would see battle again, but not until the following day. It was the evening of June 2, and many of the men of the Army of the Potomac knew what lay ahead. They prepared for their deaths by pinning scraps of paper to their uniforms so they could be easily identified later. One soldier, certain of his fate, wrote, a final entry in his diary, as noted by historian Geoffrey Ward: "June 3. Cold Harbor. I was killed."

On June 3, Grant again ordered the attack at Cold Harbor. Launched at 4:30 A.M., the boom of the cannon rattled windows in Richmond. It was a difficult assault, for Lee's positions gave Union troops little room for maneuvering; and it fell apart almost immediately. The direct frontal assault ordered by Grant was one of his worst decisions of the war. When he dispatched 50,000 men along three miles of Confederate breastworks, held by 30,000 fiery Rebels, the results were devastating. Seven thousand of Grant's men were cut down in less than 30 minutes. Lee himself was surprised at how quickly the attack fell apart. While Grant's month-long campaign had rattled Confederate confidence and brought his army to the outskirts of Richmond, the price—50,000 Union casualties—was great.

Grant could certainly not afford another Cold Harbor. Lee, too, was worried. Clifford Dowdey's *Lee* recalls Lee's words of concern to his staff in the days following Cold Harbor: "We must destroy this army of Grant's before he gets to the James River. If he gets there, it will become a siege, and then it will be a mere question of time."

Lee speaking about destroying Grant's army bordered on the illogical. Grant was receiving criticism in the North concerning his high casualties, but President Lincoln was not about to pull Grant off of Lee. Lee's forces were dwindling as well, with each loss representing one that could not be replaced immediately in the face of Grant's relentless campaign. During the weeks of fighting against Grant's forces, Lee had lost 32,000 men.

Following Cold Harbor, Grant gave Lee almost no opportunity to inflict great casualties on his army again. The Union commander would not put his army through any maneuvers that placed them directly in front of Lee's forces. Lee could not know it at the time, but Cold Harbor would prove to be his last great field victory of the war.

STALEMATE AT PETERSBURG

After weeks of fighting Lee tooth-and-nail, Grant was closer than ever to Richmond. He continued to move to his left, avoiding a direct conflict with Lee at Richmond and instead chose Petersburg as his objective, a city south of the Southern capital. Petersburg was an important supply, rail, and communications center for the Confederacy. At least five rail lines ran through the city, stretching across the South, connecting directly to Richmond. By closing off the rail lines of Petersburg, Richmond would be cut off from the rest of the Confederacy. Only 2,500 Rebel forces were in Petersburg under the command of General P.G.T. Beauregard. One well-coordinated Union attack could easily bring the fall of the southern Virginia town.

During the 10 days following Cold Harbor, Lee and Grant faced each other from entrenched positions. Then, on June 13, Grant suddenly abandoned his trenches, leaving Lee uncertain of the main Union army's whereabouts. In the meantime, the Union commander swung his men wide from Lee's positions, crossed the James River, around Richmond, and headed straight for Petersburg. By the time Lee was informed of Grant's movements, it appeared too late to stop the Union from capturing the city.

On June 15, a Union assault on Petersburg led by General W.F. "Baldy" Smith took place. While the attack had some initial success, Smith called it off, having overestimated the size of the Confederate Army holding the city. He held back, calling for reinforcements. By the third day, the possibilities of Union success in capturing Petersburg immediately had vanished. Lee had been given time to send in his own reinforcements, ensuring the Union attack would fail. In four days, Union forces outside Richmond had lost 11,000 men. Grant's total losses since launching his men into the Wilderness near Chancellorsville had mounted to 65,000, plus another 18,000 Union soldiers had left federal ranks during the spring and summer as their enlistments ran out. Regardless, Grant had lost his initial opportunity to bring about the fall of Petersburg, ensuring a lengthy siege, as Lee had feared just days earlier.

The siege unfolded as Grant ordered miles and miles of trenches built. These earthen works formed a semicircle east and south of Richmond and Petersburg. The siege of these two key Virginia cities would last for 10 months, until the end of the war. For Grant, the outcome of the war was clear. With Lee bottled up in Richmond, defending the city that had always been so dear to him, the end of the conflict was only a matter of time. As the siege continued from one month to the next, Grant was free to bring in reinforcements to maintain his military strength. Lee, however, had to spread his forces thin. As Grant had more trench lines dug, Lee had to match them as he could. Most days, Grant was satisfied with extending his lines and ordering mortar attacks into Petersburg against Confederate breastworks. On occasion, he ordered attacks along the trench lines to examine the strength of the enemy. Time was on Grant's side.

Trenches, breastworks, and other defensive works were certainly nothing knew to Robert E. Lee who had spent the early

years of his military career as a field engineer. His entrenchments at such field battle sites as Fredericksburg, Spotsylvania,
and Cold Harbor were textbook models. Now, at Petersburg
and to the north, he designed defensive works that were so
elaborate and intricate that they neutralized Grant's superior
manpower and allowed the Confederacy to continue to exist
for almost an entire year. At Petersburg, the word *siege* was
never completely accurate. In a true siege, the enemy completely surrounds its opponent and chokes off supplies, food,
or other necessities. This was never the case at Petersburg. The
true point was that Lee's army was stalemated, immobilized by
Grant, placed in a position by which Lee was not only unable
to destroy Grant's army, but was unable to accomplish anything
else, but survive.

A Man of Honor

In the meantime, the war was careening toward its inevitable end, ultimately delivering Southern defeat. Federal troops occupied the Shenandoah Valley, cutting off a significant source of food from the Rebels. Sherman's march to Atlanta succeeded, with the city in Union hands by September 2. Sherman then engaged in a "scorched earth" campaign across Georgia—his now-famous "March to the Sea"—and destroyed everything that might be used to continue the Confederate war effort. Then, in November 1864, President Lincoln was reelected to a second term. Since his Democratic challenger was none other than General George McClellan, the election was considered a Northern referendum on whether to continue the war or sue for peace. Lincoln was reelected by a larger percentage than he had been in 1860,

By 1864, 19 states had enacted provisions allowing soldiers to vote while in the field. Lincoln received 119,754 of the soldiers' votes to McClelland's 34,291, a majority of 78 percent for the incumbent president. Lincoln won the popular vote with an electoral count of 212 to 21. Pictured, Pennsylvania soldiers vote at the Army of the James headquarters in September 1864.

and the vote among his troops in his favor amounted to 78 percent! The war would go on.

THE APPROACHING END

In December, with his army badly stretched and facing daily desertions, General Lee went into Richmond and conferred with the Confederate Congress. Douglas Southall Freeman in *R.E. Lee* notes Lee's disappointment after making a strong appeal to Southern leaders for help. Lee later told one of his sons: "Well, I have been up to see the Congress and they do not seem to be able to do anything except to eat peanuts and chew tobacco, while my army is starving."

Indeed, his army was struggling to survive. Federal troops had, slowly but surely, cut off railroad lines into Petersburg, as well as road access. Elsewhere, the news of the war for Lee was equally grim. By late December, Sherman had captured Savannah, Georgia, and the seizure of Columbia, South Carolina, followed on February 17, 1865. A week later Union troops from Nashville, Tennessee, arrived by rail and captured Wilmington, the only major North Carolina port not under Union control. Sherman knew he was having as much impact on the Confederacy as had Grant's siege of Petersburg. In the face of these developments, Lee tried to keep up emotional appearances for his men. Captain John Esten Cooke, a member of Lee's staff, wrote in his book, *A Life of General Robert E. Lee*, of the importance of Lee as a symbol of endurance to his men:

> His countenance seldom, if ever, exhibited the least traces of anxiety, but was firm, hopeful, and encouraged those around him in the belief that he was still confident of success . . . The troops followed him with their eyes, or their cheers, whenever he appeared, feeling a singular sense of confidence from the presence of the gray-haired soldier in his plain uniform, and assured that, as long as Lee led them, the cause was safe.

But reality was catching up with Lee and his army. In January 1865, the U.S. Congress passed the Thirteenth Amendment to the Constitution, which called for an end to slavery. Meanwhile, in desperation, the Confederate Congress passed a bill allowing blacks to enlist in the Confederate Army. (The Union had been using black troops since 1863.) The move was a last ditch effort to save the Rebel military from collapse. The idea had been supported by Lee, who argued, according to James Robertson's *Virginian Soldier, American Citizen*, that using black troops might decide the survival of the Confederacy altogether:

> We must decide whether slavery shall be extinguished by our enemies, and the slaves used against us, or use them ourselves at the risk of the effects which may be produced upon our social institutions. My own opinion is that we should employ them without delay . . . The Negroes, under proper circumstances, will make efficient soldiers. . . . Those who are employed should be freed. It would be neither just nor wise . . . to require them to serve as slaves.

Lee's Army of Northern Virginia had reached its breaking point. This army, a force that had fought valiantly, tenaciously, and with honor, had reached its final showdown. This army had seen some of the hardest fighting of the war, as had its Northern counterpart, the Army of the Potomac. During four years of fighting, these armies had fought 10 of the 14 bloodiest battles of the war. Forty of the 50 Southern regiments that had sustained the highest percentage of casualties had fought in Virginia. Now, in the war's final days, the Union's Potomac army, under Grant's direction and leadership, was about to render utter destruction on the vestiges of General Lee's loyal Army of Northern Virginia.

THE END OF THE LINE

Lee defended Petersburg and Richmond against Grant for more than nine agonizing months. As he watched his ranks dwindle, Lee had at least three options open to him, though the first two—to retreat west or to release his army to guerrilla warfare—were never tasteful to him. To retreat west would mean abandoning his beloved Confederate capital and homeland. As commander of a "Christian army," he could not allow his men to fight in unorganized guerrilla bands outside the rules of war. This left him with the only real option—to remain in the trenches with the hope that he would be reinforced, that Grant would make a serious misstep, or that Union resolve would flag and a peace settlement negotiated.

In late March 1865, desperate to keep his army together, Lee made the decision to flee west, hoping to catch up with General Joseph Johnston's men in North Carolina and unite the two armies. Before that, he would attack the Union's position along its defensive line at Fort Stedman. The attack on March 25 failed, as Grant moved decisively, even after having been surprised. This attack soon placed Grant on the offensive, setting off a chain of events that would bring about the end of Lee's army. On March 29, Grant sent Federal troops toward Five Forks, southwest of Petersburg. The following day, Phil Sheridan's cavalry attacked Confederate positions around Five Forks. Hurriedly, Lee sent General George Pickett with five brigades to stop the Union assault. On March 31, Pickett's men forced Sheridan to abandon his positions and move back. But Union reinforcements were called in, and Sheridan recaptured Five Forks on the evening of April 1. The Confederates had no reinforcements to rely on.

Grant then ordered a complete assault at all points against Confederate trenches and breastworks for the following day. Throughout the night of April 1, Union artillerymen poured heavy fire against enemy lines. At 4:45 A.M. on April 2, massive infantry assaults were underway. Grant's troops attacked thinly held Confederate lines. Outer forts collapsed. A steady stream of Lee's men were taken prisoner. By noon on April 2, the entire first line of Confederate trenches had been captured, with only two exceptions. A belated Union assault brought down one, as Confederate troops abandoned the other. Despite Lee's efforts to recapture the lost positions, his men were ineffectual. During the fighting, General A.P. Hill was killed. Twelve hours after the Union attacks began, the Confederate positions around Petersburg had been overwhelmed. Federal troops moved north toward Richmond, nearly four years after General Irwin McDowell had marched his forces south toward Richmond, engaging the young Confederacy at Bull Run.

THE DESTRUCTION OF RICHMOND

As Union forces overwhelmed Confederate defenses at Petersburg, President Jefferson Davis was attending worship at St. Paul's Episcopal Church. There he received a telegram from General Lee informing him that Richmond must be abandoned. By nightfall, the Rebel leader and his cabinet took a train out of Richmond to the west, leaving the capital without leadership, and the Confederacy with a government on the run.

Word of approaching Union forces caused panic in the streets of Richmond. Officials began destroying government records. Others grabbed archival documents and fled. Still other government officers snatched the treasury's remaining gold and headed out of the city. Citizens crowded the railroad station, desperate to escape. Facilities throughout the city were put to the torch, not by Union men, but by Confederates, intending to destroy any depots of supplies the advancing Yankees might capture. At the docks, Confederates blew up their ironclads. Barrels of oil-soaked material were poured out on bridges and set on fire.

Soon, Richmond was ablaze. Starving citizens pillaged the city, stormed into government storage facilities, and made off with any food they could get their hands on. Storehouses of ammunition caught fire and 750,000 shells exploded, killing people on the streets and in their homes. By the morning of April 3, a thick cloud of smoke hung over the city, blocking the sun. That evening, the first Union troops entered Richmond and began putting out fires and placing military control over the civilian population. Among the Union forces brought in to work as firemen and military policemen were the black soldiers of the 25th Corps.

As Richmond came under Union control, the Army of Northern Virginia moved quickly west with Union forces at their heels. Meade's 2nd and 6th Corps, along with Sheridan's cavalry and the 5th Corps, followed closely behind. Lee's men could only move so fast. They were starving, with no food in sight. While Lee had ordered a trainload of food to Amelia Court House, 30 miles southwest of Richmond, when the men gathered at the courthouse on April 4 to be fed, they discovered the train had been rerouted. For the next 24 hours, Lee sent his men to forage for food, causing him to lose a day of retreat.

Once the Army of Northern Virginia resumed its retreat, Union forces were at every turn. Lee continued to push his men west toward the Appalachian Mountains, abandoning any hope of meeting up with Joseph Johnston's men. Then, 10 miles out of Farmville, Lee's rearguard was struck by Sheridan's men. The battle of Sayler's Creek, fought on April 6, resulted in the capture of 7,000 Confederates, including 6 Rebel generals. Two days later, Sheridan cut off the retreating Confederate Army near Appomattox Court House. By nightfall, Lee's men were trapped after having escaped from Petersburg just a week earlier.

Despite their precarious position, the Army of Northern Virginia struck out against the Union left flank on April 9. While Sheridan's cavalry fell back, Union infantry came forward with artillery and halted the Confederate assault. Hemmed in at every turn, surrounded by ever-increasing numbers of blue-clad Federals, Lee faced his destiny. There was no choice but to surrender. Despite pleas from his men to hold on, to allow his men to disperse and fight a guerrilla war, Lee knew what he had to do. Historian Douglas Southall Freeman recalls Lee's words in *R.E. Lee: A Biography*, "There is nothing left for me but to go and see General Grant," said Lee to his staff, "and I would rather die a thousand deaths."

THE SURRENDER

Grant and Lee had been in communication since April 7. On that day, Grant had requested Lee's surrender. Lee refused, asking instead for a negotiated peace. Grant replied that he had no authority to discuss the issue of peace, but if it was peace the Southern general wanted, he could hurry it along by ordering his men to disarm. Lee rejected the offer. Two days later, with no way out and his men tired and hungry, Lee sent word to Grant he would like to discuss surrender. Both armies were informed of the meeting and an immediate armistice began as blue and gray soldiers put aside their weapons and truce flags flew in both camps.

Lee and his military secretary, Colonel Charles Marshall, rode into the small Virginia town of Appomattox Court House with its couple dozen houses in the company of one of Grant's staff officers. A private home belonging to Wilmer McLean was selected as the meeting place. Lee arrived first wearing a brand-new uniform purchased for him by some supporters in England. A new, bejeweled sword hung at his side. Grant reached the McLean home at 1:30 P.M., wearing a private's uniform (as he often did) splattered with mud. He had ridden 35 miles that morning to meet with Lee. Only the stars on his shoulders indicated his rank. He carried no sword.

Outside the house, Grant tied up his horse, Cincinnati, next to Lee's mount, Traveller. Once inside, the two men talked only briefly, sitting about 10 feet opposite each other. Grant reminded Lee that they had met once before, during the Mexican War. Lee remembered the encounter, he said, but stated he could not remember what Grant looked like. The two men spoke of the Mexican conflict, talked about the weather. A dozen Union officers, including Sheridan and young George Armstrong Custer, stood in the room, listening. Finally, Lee turned Grant to the business at hand. Historian Gene Smith notes Lee's words: "I suppose, General Grant, that the object of our present meeting is fully understood. I asked to see you to ascertain upon what terms you would receive the surrender of my army."

Grant's terms were, under the circumstances, generous. All Lee's men were to be accounted for and a list provided to Grant. All surrendering Confederates were to be paroled prisoners.

All materials of war, except for side arms, horses, and the personal effects of the officers, were to be surrendered. Each Rebel soldier was, as noted by historian Emory Thomas, "allowed to return to his home, not to be disturbed by the United States authorities so long as they observe their paroles." Since the surrender agreement allowed Confederate officers to retain their side arms, Lee did not have to surrender his sword to General Grant, as would otherwise have been the custom.

Lee accepted the terms and thanked Grant for his generosity. As a copy of the terms was penned by a Union officer, Grant offered Lee 25,000 rations to feed his starving army. The Confederate general accepted. The rations were among those Union forces had captured from a Confederate train days earlier. Once the documents were completed, Lee signed them. By then, the hour was approaching 4 P.M. Lee rose, as did Grant. The two warriors shook hands. The Confederate general bowed to the other Union officers in the room. He picked up his hat and gloves, and walked out of the room, where he was saluted by several Federal officers on McLean's front porch. As Lee mounted his horse, Grant and his men came out of the house to watch him off. Grant took off his hat, and his men did the same. Lee removed his hat, and rode away.

When Lee returned to his army, his men cheered him, then fell silent. As related by *Lee and Grant*, one asked him, "General, are we surrendered?" Lee told him: "Men, we have fought the war together, and I have done the best I could for you." His aging, patrician voice cracked with emotion. "You will all be paroled and go to your homes." Tears filled Lee's eyes. His voice made no more sound, but his lips formed his final word to his men, those who had served him faithfully through hardship and sacrifice: "Good-bye."

Forty years had passed since young Robert E. Lee had entered the halls of West Point. During this time, he had worn two military uniforms, one blue and the other gray. He had served both the armies of the United States and of the

The deadliest American war in history came to an end on April 9, 1865, after Lee surrendered his Army of Northern Virginia to Grant at Appomattox Court House. More than a half million soldiers died along with an undetermined number of civilians. The day after his surrender, Lee delivered his farewell address to his army.

Confederate States of America. Lee had struggled as his men had struggled; fought as his men had fought. He had seen more death and destruction than most men ever live to see. But it was all over now. He would put aside his uniform, return to civilian life, and try and put the past four years behind him.

LAST YEARS

Although at the end of the war Robert E. Lee was only 58 years old, he had aged in appearance beyond his years. Following his surrender on behalf of his army, he soon returned to his beloved Richmond with Mary. He found the Virginia capital in ruins, burned out by retreating Confederates. Lee was greeted by thousands of his fellow Southerners in the city, who did not cheer him, but remained silent as he passed, out of respect. As he rode Traveller through the crowds, Lee repeatedly tipped his hat and bowed his head.

He was now a man without a home and without a job. Much of Virginia was desolate from the effects of war, yet Lee remained in his home state. He gathered his family around him and soon began to speak out for healing and recovery, not bitterness and hate. Instead of looking to the past, he set his eyes on the future for himself and his fellow Southerners. He even encouraged an end to segregation during worship services at St. Paul's Episcopal Church in Richmond.

Richmond became too chaotic and noisy for Lee. He could not even go out for a walk without crowds of people following him, so he took his strolls at night. Lee and his wife moved to a small house on a plantation along the banks of the James River provided by a widowed family friend. In a short time, Lee was considering his first offer of employment. In September 1865, the trustees of Washington College in Lexington, Virginia, asked Lee if would be interested in serving as the college's president. The school was not prestigious, and the campus buildings had been partially destroyed by rampaging Federal soldiers in 1864. In 1865, only 45 male students were still in attendance, along with 4 faculty members. The trustees thought Lee would bring a new respect to Washington College and that his participation could help with their planned fundraising campaign.

Lee was uncertain about taking the job at first. He had served as director of West Point and it had not been a pleasant experience. Also, he was not certain his reputation would prove to be a positive influence on the school. The college presidency would not pay well, but friends encouraged him and he accepted the offer. As historian Al Kaltman notes, Lee stated his primary goal in taking the academic post: "I have a self-imposed task which I must accomplish. I have led the young men of the South in battle; I have seen many of them die on the field; I shall devote my remaining energies to training young men to do their duty in life."

Lee was hands-on, meeting with each student to get to know him personally. The college recovered from the upheaval caused by war. New England minister, Henry Ward Beecher—who had campaigned for an end to slavery before the war—helped Lee raise money for the college. Cyrus McCormick, famous for inventing the mechanical reaping machine, became one of Washington College's greatest benefactors. Before the end of Lee's first year as president, fund-raising efforts had produced $100,000 in support for the college, and the student body doubled to over 100, with another 10 faculty members added.

Lee remained busy with his post—revamping the curriculum, working to establish a new law school on campus, and overseeing the building of a new chapel. Lee always considered the moral and religious teachings at the college to be of the utmost importance. According to Gene Smith's *Lee and Grant*, Lee once told the college's professor of moral philosophy: "Oh, Doctor, if I could only know that all of the young men in the college were good Christians, I should have nothing more to desire!" When he spoke those words, he broke down and cried.

As part of the old Virginian's leadership of the college, Lee also changed the punishment system for his students. Lee replaced the paddle with an honor system. He would sit down and talk with the boys who broke the college's rules. According to William Jones's *Life and Letters of Robert Edward Lee*, at least one student did not like the new punishment system: "I wish he had whipped me. I could have stood it better. But he talked to me so kindly, and so tenderly, about my mother, and the sacrifices which she, a widow, is making to send me to college, and of how I ought to appreciate her love . . . that the first thing I knew I was blubbering like a baby."

As tirelessly as Lee worked on behalf of the college, he also worked to help restore his formerly divided country. He testified several times before congressional committees in Washington,

D.C., where he could look to the west and see Arlington, his former home. When General Grant was elected president of the United States in 1868, he invited Lee to the White House. The aging Southerner graciously accepted.

Although the U.S. government did not try Confederate soldiers for the "treason" of serving the Confederacy in war, still Lee applied for a pardon. Unfortunately, due to government bureaucracy, Lee's request was lost, only to be found in 1975. Only then, more than a century after the war, was the South's greatest general pardoned by Congress.

Lee remained at Washington College for the rest of his life, which was another five years. They were days filled with both sadness and joy. He enjoyed being with his family, which included his three surviving daughters (none of whom ever married), and his beloved horse, Traveller. Lee and Traveller took regular rides and even stopped by the Lexington cemetery where he visited the grave of his faithful comrade-in-arms— Stonewall Jackson.

THE APPROACH OF DEATH

Lee was receding into the twilight years of his life. In 1869, Lee's fifth year at Washington College, the student body numbered 400 students, and the school employed 20 professors. Lee was a forward-thinker, having added chemistry, metallurgy, astronomy, architecture, mechanical and civil engineering, and modern languages to the curriculum. Washington College was the first school of professional journalism education in the country, and he added both a business school and a law school to the curriculum. He also had plans to add the study of photography and finance.

Gene Smith's *Lee and Grant* recounts a story of Lee visiting a resort during his fifth year as the college's president. That evening, at dinner, the old warrior shared a conversation with a young Southern woman who felt several Northerners in the room were mocking the Southerners present. When Lee told her that such bitterness toward the South pained him, the young girl asked him a pointed question.

"But, General Lee," she asked, "did you never feel resentment to the North?"

Lee's answer revealed the inherent and true nature of the old Virginian.

"I believe I may say, looking into my own heart, and speaking as in the presence of God, that I have never known one moment of bitterness or resentment." These were true words for Lee, the gentleman from Virginia, the soldier of the South. Even when given the opportunity, he would not nurse grudges or brood about the war. On one occasion, Lee was in hearing of a faculty member who spoke unflatteringly about Grant, who was then running for president of the United States. The remarks immediately raised Lee's ire. In words related by historian Charles Flood, Lee said: "Sir, if you ever again presume to speak disrespectfully of General Grant in my presence, either you or I will sever his connection with this university."

At the beginning of the academic year in 1869 Lee's health turned. The problem that had plagued him during the war—a heart condition—caught up with him at last. He struggled that semester with difficulties in breathing and was often bedridden. By the spring of 1870, he took a tour of the South hoping to improve his health. The trip gave him the opportunity to revisit with old friends and return to places that had been a part of his younger years. The grand old man of the Confederacy sat for an oil portrait as well as a marble statue.

Lee returned to his beloved Washington College. That fall, while praying at the family table at dinner, Lee suffered a stroke on September 28, 1870, which left him partially paralyzed. Two weeks later, on October 12, Robert E. Lee—husband, father, engineer, Christian soldier, college president, and stoic symbol of a South that had died the day he surrendered at Appomattox—died at 9:30 in the morning.

Today, Lee is admired for his loyalty and character, and military historians study the tactical maneuvers he used in battle against stronger contenders. This painting by Frank Buchser hangs in the Swiss embassy in Washington, D.C., and was the last to be completed in his lifetime. He is not posed in uniform, signifying his desire to leave the war in the past.

Across the country Americans mourned the passing of the gallant general. Newspapers extolled his virtues. His college mourned him and the trustees immediately renamed the school Washington and Lee University. Even today, many students refer to the alma mater as "General Lee's College." It is there that Lee was put to rest in a tomb in the new chapel's basement, known as Lee's Chapel. A statue of Lee rests above his tomb, a marble image of a uniformed Lee sleeping in his tent on a heavily draped cot. His wife, Mary, who died three years after her husband, is buried next to him.

Although Lee was just 63 years old, he had managed to leave his mark. His was a complicated legacy of heroism and principled values, of honor and the virtues of a Christian gentleman. He had supported a new nation founded on ideals that were not exactly his own, by taking up a sword forged of loyalty. In peace he had taken up the banner of kinship and brotherhood. No man in America could have led the South better, and no man of the South better represented the humble voice of reconciliation after the war than Robert E. Lee.

1807 Robert Edward Lee is born on January 19.

1818 Lee's father, Lighthorse Harry Lee, dies when young Robert is only 11.

1825 Lee receives an appointment to attend West Point.

1829 Lee graduates from West Point and soon takes up duties as an army engineer. Lee's mother dies the same year.

1831 Lee marries Mary Anne Randolph Custis.

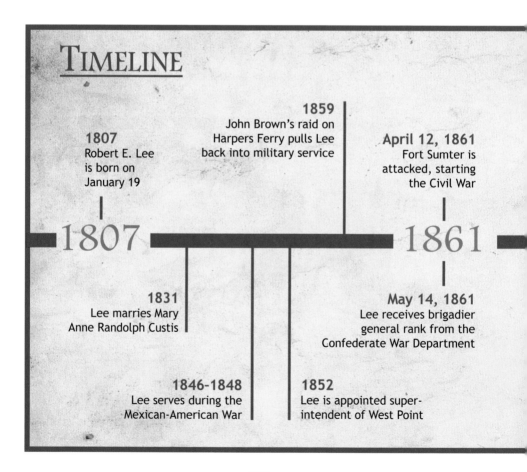

TIMELINE

1807
Robert E. Lee is born on January 19

1859
John Brown's raid on Harpers Ferry pulls Lee back into military service

April 12, 1861
Fort Sumter is attacked, starting the Civil War

1807 — **1861**

1831
Lee marries Mary Anne Randolph Custis

May 14, 1861
Lee receives brigadier general rank from the Confederate War Department

1846-1848
Lee serves during the Mexican-American War

1852
Lee is appointed superintendent of West Point

1832   The Lees' first child, George Washington Custis Lee, is born in September.

1835   The Lees' second child, Mary, is born.

1837   Lee is assigned to St. Louis where he is to keep the Mississippi River from veering away from St. Louis. The Lees' third child, William Henry Fitzhugh, is born.

1839   Daughter Ann is born.

1841   Lee is transferred to New York where he works for the next five years. His daughter Agnes is born.

1843   Robert Jr. is born.

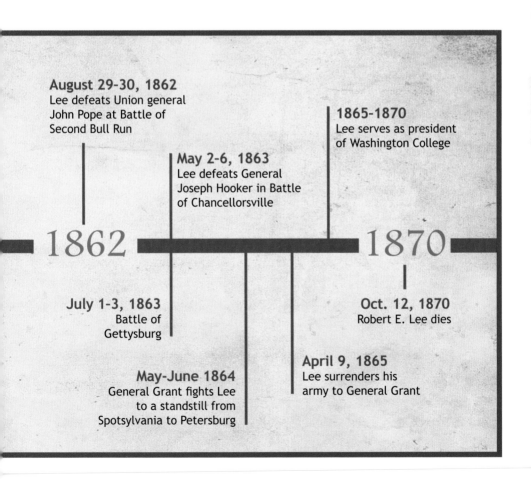

August 29-30, 1862
Lee defeats Union general John Pope at Battle of Second Bull Run

1865-1870
Lee serves as president of Washington College

May 2-6, 1863
Lee defeats General Joseph Hooker in Battle of Chancellorsville

1862   1870

July 1-3, 1863
Battle of Gettysburg

Oct. 12, 1870
Robert E. Lee dies

May-June 1864
General Grant fights Lee to a standstill from Spotsylvania to Petersburg

April 9, 1865
Lee surrenders his army to General Grant

1845   The Lees' last child, Mildred, is born.

1846-1848 Lee serves during the Mexican-American War.

1849   Lee is assigned to engineering duties in Baltimore.

1852   Lee is appointed as the superintendent of West Point Military Academy.

1855   Lee is appointed to serve with the 2nd Calvary in Texas.

1857   When Lee's father-in-law dies, Robert leaves the military to serve as executor and to restore Arlington.

1859   John Brown's raid on Harpers Ferry pulls Lee back into military service. Lee brings about Brown's capture.

1860   Lee returns to Texas to take command of the 2nd Cavalry.

1861   **April 12** Fort Sumter is attacked, starting the Civil War.

             April 18 Lee is approached to take command of U.S. Army following attack on Fort Sumter, which Lee refuses.

             April 21 Lee accepts offer to organize defense of Virginia.

             May 14 Lee receives brigadier general rank from the Confederate War Department.

             July 21 First major battle of the Civil War, Bull Run, is fought. Lee does not fight directly.

             Sept. 10–14 Lee loses his first military engagement of the Civil War, the Battle of Cheat Mountain.

1862   **May 31** Lee becomes commander of Army of Northern Virginia after General Joseph Johnston is severely wounded in Battle of Seven Pines.

             Jun. 25–Jul. 1 Lee engages General McClellan during the Battles of the Seven Days.

August 29–30 Lee defeats Union general John Pope at Battle of Second Bull Run.

September 17 Lee is checkmated by General McClellan during the Battle of Antietam (Sharpsburg), forcing Lee to retreat back into Virginia.

October 20 Lee's daughter Agnes dies of typhoid fever.

December 11 Lee defeats General Ambrose Burnside in the Battle of Fredericksburg.

1863   **May 2–6** Lee defeats General Joseph Hooker in Battle of Chancellorsville.

June 3 Lee orders his men to begin march into Pennsylvania, taking the war offensively into the North.

July 1–3 Battle of Gettysburg takes place, resulting in the defeat of Lee's army.

1864   **May 5–12** Lee and Grant engage one another for the first time during battles in the Wilderness and at Spotsylvania. Both armies inflict significant casualties.

May–June Grant fights Lee to a standstill from Spotsylvania to Petersburg, ending with Lee trapped in Petersburg, leading to a nine-month siege.

1865   **March 25** Lee orders attack on Union lines at Petersburg before abandoning trenches and fleeing with his army to the west. The attack is repulsed.

April 9 Lee surrenders his army to General Grant.

1865-1870   Lee serves as president of Washington College.

1870   **Oct. 12** Robert E. Lee dies.

1873   Mary Lee dies.

GLOSSARY

abolitionism   The movement to end and prohibit slavery.

aide-de-camp   A military officer who serves a commanding officer in his headquarters.

aristocratic   Refers to those members of the upperclass.

arroyos   A small, steep-sided gulch with a nearly flat floor, usually found in the Southwest.

"Bleeding Kansas"   A series of violent events involving proslavery and anti-slavery people that took place in Kansas territory and the state of Missouri between 1854 and 1858.

breastworks   A low, sometimes hastily built wall for defense, which typically stands chest high.

brevet   A "temporary" advancement in military rank, often made in the field without official approval.

demerit   A negative mark against a person for misconduct.

desertion   To abandon; to leave the ranks of an army without permission.

emancipation   The act of freeing individuals from service or slavery.

executor   A person designated to carry out the duties or provisions of a will when someone dies.

Federals   Troops who fought for the Union during the Civil War.

Federalists   An early American political party led by Alexander Hamilton who typically supported strong national government at the expense of the power of the various states. The party largely ceased to exist following the War of 1812.

flank   Either end of a line of massed soldiers, signified as an army's left or right.

guerrilla Fighting done without the benefit of an organized, official military structure or system.

invalidism The condition of having prolonged illness or disability.

Kansas-Nebraska Act An 1854 act of Congress that created the territories of Kansas and Nebraska.

land speculation The practice of purchasing large tracts of land at a low price and making a profit by subdividing that land and selling it in smaller parcels at a higher price.

mess hall A facility at a military post or base where meals are taken.

minie ball A cone-shaped projectile fired in a musket or rifle, invented by French army captain, Claude Minie.

mortar Heavy, short cannon designed to lob large shells in a high arc over a short distance against enemy fortifications. Often used during sieges.

pedregal The prehistoric, volcanic lava bed located southeast of modern-day Mexico City.

peninsula A portion of land surrounded on most sides by water.

picket A forward position on a battlefield meant to serve as a watch on an enemy's advance.

pontoon boats Flat-bottomed boats used to create a floating bridge across a river or stream. Such boats were placed side-by-side, attached together, then covered over with planking to create a workable passageway for soldiers, artillery, horses, and wagons.

popular sovereignty The political theory that encourages the residents of a Western territory to vote whether or not they want slavery to exist in their future state.

Rebels Term for Southerners who supported the Confederacy during the Civil War.

referendum   A vote taken by the people that reflects their will or level of support.

regiment   A unit of an army made up of several battalions or squadrons of soldiers organized into one large group, usually commanded by a colonel. It is smaller than a brigade.

"scorched earth"   A military practice of destroying an enemy's physical assets to reduce an enemy's capacity to wage war.

secede   To withdraw formally from an alliance, a federation, or association.

sharpshooter   A expert rifleman capable of firing accurately at targets from great distances.

Shenandoah Valley   A fertile valley stretching north to south in western Virginia which lies west of the Blue Ridge Mountains.

shore batteries   Groupings of cannon or artillery situated along a coast.

siege   The act of surrounding a fortified place by an army trying to capture it.

skirmish   A small-scale military engagement with less scope or action than a full-fledged battle.

Special Order # 191   A set of orders issued by Robert E. Lee in the spring of 1862, which called for his forces to be divided and dispatched in several directions.

subordinate   An enlisted man serving under an officer of higher rank.

tariffs   Fees placed on foreign goods entering another country.

Tidewater   The region of the Chesapeake Bay, including Maryland and eastern Virginia, where coastal rivers are affected by the tides.

Valley Campaign   A Confederate campaign led by General Stonewall Jackson into the Shenandoah Valley during the spring of 1862—its purpose being to distract several Union armies simultaneously—keeping them from advancing on Richmond.

BIBLIOGRAPHY

Alexander, Bevin. *Robert E. Lee's Civil War*. Holbrook, Mass.: Adams Media Corporation, 1998.

Basler, Roy P., ed. *The Collected Works of Abraham Lincoln*, 9 vols. New Brunswick, N.J.: Rutgers University Press, 1953.

Carmichael, Peter S., ed. *Audacity Personified: The Generalship of Robert E. Lee*. Baton Rouge: Louisiana State University Press, 2004.

Cooke, John Esten. *A Life of General Robert E. Lee*. New York: D. Appleton, 1871.

Dabney, Robert L. *Life and Campaigns of Lieut.-Gen. Thomas J. Jackson*. New York: Blalock & Co., 1866.

Dowdey, Clifford. *Lee*. New York: Bonanza Books, 1965.

Earle, Peter. *Robert E. Lee*. New York: Saturday Review Press, 1973.

Flood, Charles Bracelen. *Lee: The Last Years*. Boston: Houghton Mifflin Company, 1981.

Foote, Shelby. *The Civil War, A Narrative, Volume 3: Yorktown to Cedar Mountain*. Alexandria, Va.: Time-Life Books, 1999.

Freeman, Douglas Southall. *Lee of Virginia*. New York: Charles Scribner's Sons, 1958.

———. *R.E. Lee: A Biography*. New York: Charles Scribner's Sons, 1934-35.

Horn, Stanley F., ed. *The Robert E. Lee Reader*. New York: Grossett & Dunlap, 1949.

Johnson, R.U. and C. C. Buel, eds. *Battles and Leaders of the Civil War*. New York: Century Company, 1887–1888, Volume II.

Jones, J. William. *Life and Letters of Robert Edward Lee, Soldier and Man*. New York: Neale, 1906.

Journals and Papers of the Virginia State Convention of 1861. Richmond: Virginia State Library, 1961–1966), Volume 1 (1961).

Kaltman, Al. *The Genius of Robert E. Lee: Leadership Lessons for the Outgunned, Outnumbered and Underfinanced.* Paramus, N.J.: Prentice Hall Press, 2000.

McClellan, George B. *The Civil War Papers of George B. McClellan.* New York: Ticknor & Fields, 1989.

McPherson, James M. *Ordeal by Fire: The Civil War and Reconstruction.* New York: McGraw-Hill, 1992.

Nevins, Allan. *The War for the Union: The Organized War 1863-64.* New York: Charles Scribner's Sons, 1971.

Pender, William Dorsey. *The General to his Lady.* Chapel Hill: University of North Carolina Press, 1962.

Reid, Brian Holden. *Robert E. Lee: Icon for a Nation.* London: Weidenfeld & Nicolson, 2005.

Rice, Earle. *Robert E. Lee: First Soldier of the Confederacy.* Greensboro, N.C.: Morgan Reynolds, 2005.

Robertson, James. *Virginian Soldier, American Citizen: Robert E. Lee.* New York: Atheneum Books, 2005.

Roland, Charles P. *Reflections on Lee: An Assessment.* Mechanicsburg, Penn.: Stackpole Books, 1993.

Sears, Stephen W. *Landscape Turned Red: The Battle of Antietam.* New York: Houghton Mifflin, 1983.

Smith, Gene. *Lee and Grant.* New York: Penguin Group, 1984

Thomas, Emory M. *Robert E. Lee, A Biography.* New York: W. W. Norton & Company, 1995.

Ward, Geoffrey. *The Civil War: An Illustrated History.* New York: Random House, 1990.

Wilkins, J. Steven. *Call of Duty: The Sterling Nobility of Robert E. Lee.* Nashville: Cumberland House Publishing, 1997.

FURTHER RESOURCES

BOOKS

Anderson, Paul Christopher. *Robert E. Lee: Legendary Commander of the Confederacy*. New York: Rosen Publishing Group, 2001.

Arnold, James R. *On to Richmond: The Civil War in the East, 1861-62*. Minneapolis: Lerner Publishing Group, 2001.

Bradford, Gamaliel. *Lee the American*. San Diego: Dover Publications, 2004.

Carter, E. J. *Robert E. Lee*. Portsmouth, N.H.: Heinemann, 2004.

Gillis, Jennifer Blizin. *Robert E. Lee: Confederate Commander*. Mankato, Minn.: Coughlan Publishing, 2005.

Grabowski, Patricia A. *Robert E. Lee: Confederate General*. Philadelphia: Chelsea House Publishers, 2000.

Hale, Sarah Elder. *Gettysburg: Bold Battle in the North*. Peterborough, N.H.: Cobblestone, 2005.

———. *Robert E. Lee: Duty and Honor*. Peterborough, N.H.: Cobblestone Publishing Company, 2005.

Kantor, MacKinlay. *Lee and Grant at Appomattox*. New York: Sterling Publishing, 2007.

Kay, Alan N. *Crossroads at Gettysburg*. Shippensburg, Penn.: White Mane Publishing Company, 2005.

McLeese, Don. *Robert E. Lee*. Vero Beach, Fla.: Rourke Publishing, 2005.

Monroe, Judy. *Robert E. Lee*. Mankato, Minn.: Coughlan Publishing, 2002.

Ransom, Candice F. *Robert E. Lee*. Minneapolis: Lerner Publishing Group, 2006.

WEB SITES

Aldie's Civil War: Robert E. Lee
    http://www.us-civilwar.com/lee.htm

Arlington House, The Robert E. Lee Memorial
    http://www.nps.gov/arho/

Shotgun's Home of the American Civil War: Robert E. Lee
    http://www.civilwarhome.com/leebio.htm

Son of the South
    http://www.sonofthesouth.net/leefoundation/About%20the
        %20General.htm

Stratford Hall
    http://www.stratfordhall.org

United States Civil War Photographs
    http://usa-civil-war.com/Lee/lee.html

Virtual War Museum: U.S. Civil War Hall—Robert E. Lee
    http://www.robertelee.org/

PICTURE CREDITS

⚔ INDEX ⚔

# ABOUT THE AUTHOR

TIM MCNEESE is associate professor of history at York College in York, Nebraska, where he is in his seventeenth year of college instruction. Professor McNeese earned an associate of arts degree from York College, a bachelor of arts in history and political science from Harding University, and a master of arts in history from Missouri State University. A prolific author of books for elementary, middle and high school, and college readers, McNeese has published more than 100 books and educational materials over the past 20 years, on everything from the founding of early New York to Hispanic authors. His writing has earned him a citation in the library reference work, *Contemporary Authors* and multiple citations in *Best Books for Young Teen Readers*. In 2006, Tim appeared on the History Channel program, *Risk Takers, History Makers: John Wesley Powell and the Grand Canyon*. He was a faculty member at the 2006 Tony Hillerman Writers Conference in Albuquerque. His wife, Beverly, is an assistant professor of English at York College. They have two married children, Noah and Summer, and three grandchildren, Ethan, Adrianna, and Finn William. Tim and Bev sponsored study trips for college students on the Lewis and Clark Trail in 2003 and 2005 and to the American Southwest in 2008. You may contact Professor McNeese at tdmcneese@york.edu.